THE WAY OF THE RONIN

RIDING THE WAVES OF CHANGE

DR. BEVERLY POTTER

RONIN PUBLISHING

The Way of the Ronin
Riding the Waves of Change
ISBN: 1-57951-051-5
Copyright © 1984, 2001 Beverly A. Potter, Ph.D.

Published by
RONIN Publishing, Inc.
PO Box 522
Berkeley, CA 94701
www.roninpub.com

Credits:

Illustrations:	Matt Gouig
Cover illustration:	Matt Gouig
Cover design:	Judy July, Generic Type
Cover photo:	©1997 Digital Vision

Distributed to the trade by Publishers Group West

Printed in the United States of America by Bertelsmann

Library of Congress Card Number: 2001116521

* *Waves, Natal Coast, South Africa*

*To the free spirit
in each of us*

The Way of the Ronin is something that many in the management world have been waiting for for some time. It offers a new insight on how to bolt past the competition to corporate success and how to extracate the organization and oneself from seemingly impossible situations. And much more, as Dr. Potter skillfully integrates a wide range of material through the eyes of the *ronin*, that free spirit in an otherwise institutionalized society, for practical applications in today's confused yet regulated operations.

So chock full of enriching and effectuating ideas, harmoniously blended into a timely theme. Many, many people will relish work and enjoy life much the better from studying *The Way of the Ronin*.

—Ralph G. H. Siu
THE CRAFT OF POWER
THE MASTER MANAGER

Other Books by Docpotter

Overcoming Job Burnout
How to Renew Enthusiasm for Work

Finding a Path with a Heart
How to Go from Burnout to Bliss

Preventing Job Burnout
A Workbook

The Worrywart's Companion
21 Ways to Soothe Yourself & Worry Smart

From Conflict to Cooperation
How to Mediate a Dispute

High Performance Goal Setting
Using Intuition to Conceive & Achieve Your Dreams

Drug Testing at Work
A Guide for Employers

Pass the Test
An Employee's Guide to Drug Testing

The Healing Magic of Cannabis

Brain Boosters
Foods & Drugs that Make You Smarter

Turning Around
Keys to Motivation and Productivity

Table of Contents

PART ONE

THE FEUDAL WORKPLACE

Chapter 1

Fast Track

The big question when we were children was "What do you want to be when you grow up?" No one ever thought to ask, "What sort of life do you want to be living when you grow up?" The question assumed that the life created by following a linear path up the corporate or professional ladder would satisfy each of us.

Our task was to choose one vocational specialty, from a smorgasbord of possibilities, for our entire work lives. Without realizing it, we were set up to experience frustration and disappointment, and forced to make dramatic changes without warning or preparation. By following the linear career strategy, we've whittled ourselves down to fit a slot in an intricate system—a system that is changing in unprecedented and unpredictable ways.

To a far greater degree than we realize, our work molds our entire lives: where we live, who our friends are, how we entertain, what we do for leisure, the values we live by, and the way we think. Consequently, choice of a career becomes a necessary and fateful process, because in choosing an occupation, we also select an identity and a way of life.

So we went to college to become teachers, lawyers, or business managers. Or we entered technical school to learn a trade. And once made, this educational training commitment became our vocation for life. We were expected to follow a strictly linear career path within the organizations where we worked. After an appropriate number of years of shopping around, we were to settle down into a corporate family and build a career. We were expected to be established on our career path by our late twenties, certainly no later than our early thirties. Then we were to advance up the promotional ladder.

It was in moving from trainee up the various rungs toward the top that we were expected to achieve success and satisfy our needs for esteem and personal growth. During the Post-WWII Growth Era, following this linear strategy made it relatively easy for a young professional to ride the growth curve all the way to the top. Jobs were plentiful, especially at the top of the occupational career ladder. The need for highly prestigious and well-paid professionals grew faster than the need for any other category of worker.

We Want Something More

In our youth, we enjoyed affluence and possessions which we found to be nice but not satisfying. We watched our fathers in their gray flannel suits and our mothers confined to PTA meetings and coffee klatches in the suburbs. We sensed that we had been indoctrinated with a rigid understanding of success and personal growth.

We longed for work that allowed for self-expression where we could keep our individuality. So in the 1960s and 70s, we tuned in, turned on, and dropped out. We went to sensitivity groups, learned to give massages, experienced weekends at Esalen, expanded our awareness with Zen, meditated, and became assertive. Most of us dropped back in, but many did not. Some tried to be both in and out of the World Game of making an impact on mainstream businesses, professions, and society.

We Want Fuller Lives

We rejected the notion that affluence and possessions alone yield a "successful" life and we adopted new values pivoting around self-fulfillment and personal freedom. While our parents placed their emphasis on getting ahead and adjusting to the mores of the organizational structure, we questioned the traditional postwar work ethic, insisting there must be something more to life than making money, accumulating possessions, and struggling to get ahead.

We became "cultural creatives." demanding greater flexibility in our lives, with more opportunity to express ourselves and develop our potential. Increasingly, we define success and failure by our own terms and are less accepting of the external gauges that society and organizations imposed on our parents. We manifeste our desire to develop our full potential in our life-styles, in our attitudes toward work, and in a great mistrust of our large institutions and their leaders.

The baby boom transforms each institution through which it passes. The pig is now devouring the python.

—John Naisbitt

MEGATRENDS

By the turn of the Century we were riding a wave of technological breakthroughs, market openings and new product introduction. The wave carried us into the new millennium and a global economical revolution. In its wake came a boom economy. More people were making more money than ever before—and making it in shorter periods of time. Stories of dot.com and IPO instant multimillionaires were intoxicating. But no sooner did we adjust to our newly found wealth than the economy stalled.

Suddenly we realized that again have we lost track of what matters—really. We witnessed joyless workdays. We insisted that we couldn't be bought. Yet, again we traded our freedom for the seduction of money and before realizing it many of us were indentured again—by megabucks!

Questioning Redux

All over America, we are weighing the rewards of conventional success and the traditional notions of work, and finding them lacking. And to our horror, we are discovering that we are locked in. We are trapped. For too many of us, the future is dictated by choices we made in high school and college. Our specialized vocations have become comfortable cells that we cannot get out of without sacrifice to either/or choices. After years of specialization and climbing the rungs of the ladder, we find that in order to make a change we must step down and start at the bottom of yet a new ladder. We must accept a tremendous drop in pay, status, and sphere of influence or return to school for lengthy training or even drop out of the World Game altogether.

> *One can spend one's whole life climbing the ladder, only to realize it's been placed against the wrong wall.*
>
> *—Joseph Campbell*

We are told this is the price we must pay if we want something more. It is *either* a conventional career of climbing the ladder and becoming ever more specialized with fewer options *or* accepting a less lucrative but more satisfying endeavor outside of the World Game.

Some, who are locked into mortgage payments, credit cards, and the kids' college bills, would like to reach for self-realization but believe they cannot. Others, not willing to give up affluence, attempt to realize themselves part-time with hobbies or volunteer work, around the edges of their jobs. They are finding that they cannot realize their self-actualization goals at work after all. They are not free. The linear career is a master who permits little deviation from a straight line. These people are trapped in a kind of corporate feudalism!

Bill's Story

My parents worked hard. They struggled so that I could have what they never had. They expected me to become a professional. I didn't question it. It seemed like the thing to do, and law seemed like the best option. I figured I'd get a lot of respect and a lot of money. So I pushed through the grind of law school. And now I've been a lawyer for nearly a decade. It's O.K. I've done well. But I'm tired of it. It's not that I don't like it. It's just that it doesn't meet all of my needs. A lot of people think I'm a hired gun. And I don't like that and I have a hard time with the values of some of my colleagues. And then there's the paperwork, the endless, endless paperwork. Remember those dread papers we had to write in college? Well, the actual work of lawyering is comprised about 80% with writing papers—forever. We call them briefs, and memos.

When I think about my options, I get depressed. Ever since I got a PC at home, I've gotten more and more interested in web management. But when I look in the paper at the job openings, I'm not qualified. Oh, maybe with a couple courses at the local college I could talk myself into an entry-level position. And I've considered it. I really have! But, you know, I'd never get far, and I'd get only about a quarter of what I make now. The money's not that important, really. And I've got some savings. But what's the point? I may as well be pumping gas for all the impact that I'd make. Of course, I could go back to school and get a degree in engineering. But it seems like I spent a lifetime in school already. I don't want to do that again. And I'm not sure I'd be any better off after I got the degree anyway. I'd probably want to do something else after a while. No, I can't start over. It's too late for that. I guess I just have to accept law and make the best of it. And find some satisfaction playing around with a personal website. It's depressing really. I feel trapped.

We Want Self-Direction

We reject such either/or choices and challenge the once unquestioned trust in the major institutions of our society. We want more freedom from the economic power of corporate plants and office bureaucracies. We are not willing to leave our new sense of self and our new social values at home. Instead, we bring with us to the office the yearnings for flexibility, for greater freedom in thought and dress; the desire for nonfinancial rewards, recognition, and respect; and the sense of belonging and contributing. We want to find fulfillment and personal satisfaction in conventional careers, while at the same time enjoying the financial rewards that will enable us to live full and rich lives.

We are less willing to sacrifice everything for the sake of the job just to make it to the next rung on the ladder. We have higher expectations about what we are going to get from work. We expect to bring our whole selves to the job—all of our skills, our interests, our values. Increasingly we insist that work be an integral part of the whole of who we are in addition to providing an economic base for rich, full, and balanced lives. We want to be center stage in our work lives. We are rewriting the script so that self-realization rather than social conformity becomes the theme of the play.

We Want Meaning

We take our work more personally—what we do is who we are. What we want most from our work is to feel that it, and thus we, as individuals, are important. We do not want just a job; we want employment that offers challenge, growth, and fulfillment. We want to matter; to make a difference. We want to feel that what we do is important and that we are making a contribution to a meaningful objective. We want work that inspires—that fills us with spirit. We want to feel potent and filled with creative energy, doing work that fulfills the soul and makes a meaningful impact.

We Want Adventure

"Work" conjurs up images of endless days walking lockstep, doing the same thing over and over. But we want to expand and experience. We want to have fun and to be stimulated in all aspects of our lives, not just during a few hours on the weekend. We want work that is a trip ticket, a vehicle to adventure.

We Want Balance

We are less willing to continue the split between work life and personal life, less willing to sacrifice our families to the corporation, and less accepting of a fractionalized existence. We want to be full people within the context of our work.

We Want Connectedness

We look to our jobs to satisfy basic emotional needs like interconectedness and support that would have been met in other eras by family, religion, and community life. We want fulfilling relationships with our co-workers that go beyond nine-to-five.

Chapter 2

Waves of Change

 Everyone agrees that the Internet and other telecommunication advances will bring decentralization of the workplace. It's hard to say what this may mean. Futurists say that our workplace will be more spread out geographically, that we will work in smaller work units, and that we will live closer to work, perhaps within walking distance—or even work out of our homes, thereby reducing the energy expenditure of commuting. It all sounds reminiscent of the "good old days of small-town America.

Everyone agrees that there will be more flexibility, diversity, and differences, not only in the workplace itself, but also among those who work there. Rank and file workers will have opportunities to make a genuine impact. All of this sounds quite good.

We are Overspecialized

Making such a transition will not be easy, however. The industrial era, captained by organizations, believes in centralizing and demands conformity and specialized work from specialized human parts—that's us. We complied with the demands and became specialists.

Overspecialization, say biologists, is an important contributing factor in a species becoming extinct. When a species becomes overspecialized in a particular ecosystem, it can be unable to adapt to changes in the environment because it does not have the flexibility and diversity to enable it to make the transition. This is where many of us are today.

Because we followed the linear career track, our ability to adapt is impaired. Having become specialized human parts for the vast organizational machine, we are now facing a crisis of adapting to an unknown future. Indeed, we find ourselves stuck on a track headed toward oblivion.

Change is Inevitable

The most dangerous thing we can do is to rigidly resist change. The coming change is inevitable and the only option is to be open and flexible. But how can we be so when we've become specialized human parts in the organizational machine, without flexibility, without a breadth of movement, without options for alternative ways of providing for our needs?

There are alternative ways of organizing people and producing products and services, but we can't think of them because we are so locked into our existing world paradigm that all other ways of organizing are seen as totally unacceptable. The ways in which we look at the world and the ways in which work and workers are organized conform to a Newtonian worldview—everything exists in a dance of cause and effect; everything is mechanistic. So it should come as no surprise that the organization itself resembles a giant machine with disposable, replaceable human parts.

Hierarchy Will Pass Away

> We are participating not merely in the birth of a new organizational form but in the birth of a new civilization.
> —*Alvin Toffler*
> *The Third Wave*

Alvin Toffler argues that the hierarchical structure of organizations is a form that is breaking down and in the future it will not be the dominant way of organizing people at work. It is difficult to conceive of a new way of organizing people that is different from the feudal chain of command which is part of our belief system and the way we naturally structure people working together.

What we are seeing today is not simply an economic upheaval, but something far deeper, something that cannot be understood within the framework of conventional economies...." The old rules don't work any longer." What we are seeing is the general crisis of industrial capitalism.... What is happening, no more, no less, is breakdown of industrial civilization on the planet and the first fragmentary appearance of a wholly new and dramatically different social order: a superindustrial civilization that will be technological, but no longer industrial.

—Alvin Toffler
THE ECO-SPASM REPORT

Teams

In the late 20th Century a new organizational form emerged—the team. At first teams were anomalies. People from across departments, often from varying levels, were pulled together to tackle a key issue. Found to be surprisingly effective, their use proliferated, even though it was unclear where to put them on the organizational chart because they were something of a wild card.

We like working in teams because they facilitate the flow of ideas and information while giving a sense of community. The creative environment is stimulating and fast moving—well, faster that the alternative down flow found in a hierarchy, where like molasses, information moves slowly and rarely do ideas flow upward to the people with the power to implement them.

Networks

With the advent of computer networks and the Internet, it becomes possible to connect people in different ways. In contrast to the hierarchy, a network structure of organizing becomes possible—a little like the way the cells in our brains are connected. As the diagram on the next page shows, hierarchies connect individuals of equal or varying power directly. Unlike hierarchies, which tend to be static and rigid, networks are dynamic and yield infinite shapes. People can interact directly with people in different functions. Folks in marketing can work directly with those in manufacturing, for example. People at the bottom of the pyramid can communicate with those at the top.

Organizational Structure

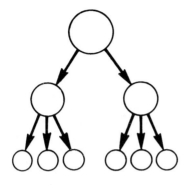 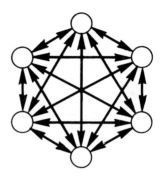

Hierarchy   Network

Add the Internet to networks and people who are not physically in the same location can connect directly. People in the New York office can interface with those in Tokyo, for example. This has many ramifications for where and how people work as well as the speed of work.

These new organizational forms are in an elementary state. The implications of these new and rapidly developing structures are left to our speculations. We literally do not know what the shape of new organizations will take. And there may not be only one.

In *Future Shock* Toffler predicts that organizations of the superindustrial society will become more and

Computer technology is the most powerful force changing human society today. Over the next generation, every man, woman, and child will have the ability to use computers for access to facts, to organizations, and—most importantly—to other human beings. There is a new type of structure that makes this access possible. It is called a network.

—*Jacques Vallee*
THE NETWORK REVOLUTION

more turbulent, filled with change. He envisions a move from bureaucracy to "adhocracy"—changing organizational forms dictated by project goals. Toffler formulated his predictions in the late 1960s. By the turn of the Century

> *The central, crucial and important business of organizations... is increasingly shifting from up and down to "sideways." What is involved in such a shift is a virtual revolution in organizational structure—and in human relations. People communicating "sideways"—i.e. to others of approximately the same level of organization—behave differently, operate under very different pressures, than those who must communicate up and down a hierarchy.*
>
> —Alvin Toffler
> FUTURE SHOCK

ad hoc projects were commonplace. They were staffed by teams made up of individuals across departments within companies, as well as across corporate borders to ally companies. Interfacing with co-workers across vast distances via email, video conferencing and the Internet were routine by 2000.

These new ways of putting people together at work are translating into a dramatic alteration in the definition of job functions. People are still differentiated, but flexibly and functionally according to skill and professional training matched to the project needs. Such changes increase the adaptability of organizations, but strain our adaptability. Will we be prepared?

E-lancers

E-lancers are electronically connected freelancers who work on project teams for a day, a week, a month, or even longer, then disperse and recombine to work on other projects. E-lancers come together on the fly to tackle a project with people who they have never met face-to-face. It all happens very fast by email. We are living the futurists' predictions. The future is now!

We're witnessing the emergency of an e-lance workplace in which a growing army of self-employed professionals use the Internet to land projects, manage hectic schedules and meet new colleagues. With telecommuting comes hope for a new way of working.

Computer networks can be used by a repressive government to look for undesirables or to flag suspects. But they can also be used by individuals to share thoughts and facts, novel ideas, visions of humanity's future destiny. They constitute communications media unparalleled in human history. And they lead us to a momentous decision.

Computer networks are going to force us in the next few years to make a choice between two types of society...the "Digital Society" and the "Grapevine Alternative."

In the Digital Society, massive amounts of computer technology are used to control people by reducing them to statistics. In the Digital Society, computers are repressive tools and their use for private communication is discouraged.

In the Grapevine Alternative, on the contrary, computers are used by people to build networks. And beyond the simple use of these networks for information we find people actually communicating through them...it will go far beyond such applications when people in large numbers discover in these networks gateways to other minds, windows to unsuspected vistas, bridges across their loneliness, and precious understanding...For the first time, a door [has] been forced open in the bureaucracy and a new type of community [is starting] to grow.

—Jacques Vallee
THE NETWORK REVOLUTION

Super-industrial Man, rather than occupying a permanent, cleanly-defined slot and performing mindless routine tasks in response to orders from above, finds increasingly that he must assume decision-making responsibility—and must do so within a kaleidoscopically changing organization structure built upon highly transient human relationships.

—Alvin Toffler
FUTURE SHOCK

That worksteads...are feasible and timely seems clear; that they are also enormously beneficial to their participants is the payoff....
Perhaps most important, the worksteader usually doesn't make a distinction between "living" and "working"... a home-based career offers the individual comfort, freedom from commuting, a sense of independence, and the opportunity to be closer to family.

—Jeremy Joan Hewes
Worksteads

E-cottages

Working for yourself doesn't mean working alone any more. Traditionally, isolation has been a downside of freelancing and entraprenuring. E-lancers on the other hand, may work alone, but they don't have to go it alone—they are part of a team. When not on a project, sometimes called "being beached," they can go online to stay in touch with people in their network and to hook another project.

What Alvin Toffler and other futurists envision is millions of people working in their homes at their PC's rather than in centralized office complexes. Such an arrangement does not require commuting or providing offices and other facilities with energy-gobbling lights and air conditioning. Yet, because of online technology, we can plug directly into the central office of the company. Indeed, it becomes possible to live in San Francisco and "work" in New York City.

Promises

A central promise of the emerging new workplace is that we can increasingly take responsibility for our work. Through these interconnections we are promised more clout, more influence to make an impact. In a *FAST Company* survey of people at work in late 1999 35% of those responding said they set their own agenda and decide the specifics of their job which is a testament that the future is arriving on schedule—perhaps a little ahead of schedule.

Opportunities for attaining what we want have never been greater. At the dawn of the 21st Century the potential for creativity and personal contribution as well as mind-boggling personal wealth for some, makes this a time of opportunity to create a kind of work life that previous generations never even imagined possible.

> *...the computer allows us to have a distinct and individually tailored arrangement with each of thousands of employees.*
> —*John Naisbitt*
> *MEGATRENDS*

Perhaps we will be saved from the totalitarian thrust of the organization, by the Internet and e-cottage. Perhaps we will have more flexible work styles, working at different times and in different ways, better integrating work and home, contending with fewer demands for conformity and not having to dress for work or having to buy all those expensive success uniforms. Perhaps it will happen; perhaps it won't. There is only one thing we can count on with absolute certainty—our futures are uncertain.

Like the *ronin* of feudal Japan, we have been cast into the waves of change. We don't know which way change will go. Perhaps we will become serfs in a new type of totalitarian organization, or perhaps the Internet will set us free. Our only security is our ability to adapt to the coming changes—even though we don't

know what they will be. The problem is that many of us are ill prepared. We are not adaptable; we are not flexible. We are specialized human parts, having prepared ourselves for one career our entire lives, a career that may soon be disintermediated.

Disintermediation

By the year 2000 the majority of the workforce was engaged in white-collar work. Even most manufacturing jobs were connected to white-collar services, including those in human resources, finance, and engineering. Tom Peters predicted that by 2015 "white-collar robots"—sophisticated software that performs and coordinates essential personnel, production, sales and accounting functions—will eliminate the majority of intermediary functions.

> *Ninety percent of white-collar jobs in the U.S. will be either destroyed or altered beyond recognition" in the first 10 to 15 years of the 21st Century.*
>
> *—Tom Peters*

Peters likens the impact on white-collar work to what forklifts, robotics and containerization did to blue-collar work in the 1960s. White-collar robots will eradicate middlemen—intermediaries—like stockbrokers, auto deals, real estate and insurance agents and mail carriers—all of which will go the way of the buggy whip. Printers will be replaced by sophisticated digital copying systems and voice recognition software will replace stenographers, executive assistance and court reporters. Even CEOs are on the chopping block, as top-down decision making becomes too cumbersome. Housekeepers will be replaced by smart appliances, and self-cleaning homes.

Chapter 3

The Company Way

 Faced with uncertainty, organizations tighten up to assert more control. It is during times of uncertainty that their feudal tendencies become most apparent. The pressures that produce conformity, however, are often misunderstood.

Conformity

The precisely interlocking processes of a complex modern society require a high degree of predictability of individual behavior. As with all feudal systems, conformity and loyalty to "The Company Way" are the primary methods of ensuring predictability. We go along with this because organizations convince us that what is good for the organization is good for us.

We conform because it seems like a sensible way to keep the organization running smoothly and keeping our jobs and comforts. In the words of William Whyte, author of the classic *The Organization Man*: "Few things are more calculated to rob the individual of his defenses than the idea that our interest and those of the organization can be wholly compatible." The conflict between the individual and society always involves the dilemma of weighting individual freedom against public safety.

The potential consequences of this direction are ominous. Many organization experts, such as Whyte, warn that because we are bound to organizations through work there is the potential for totalitarian control.

Modern organizations influence us profoundly, but so quietly that we scarcely realize that they are major agencies of social control. Our commitment to organizational roles leads us to define ourselves in terms of these roles, creating even greater potential for control. The values and attitudes of the roles we play at work spill over into all other areas of our lives. While working within the organization, we *become* what we do in the sense that our personal values increasingly match those of the organization.

Interchangeable Components

That organizations require strict obedience through the chain of command is obvious to all who work in one. Less obvious are the other mores of the organizational imperative. For example, modern organizations cannot tolerate an indispensable individual. If they did, organizations would become too dependent on such people, which is anathema to organizational thought and practice.

> *The terrible paradox is that as [we] see even more deeply into the organization, searching for security, [we] find only that [we] are the most dispensable commodity of all.*
>
> —Scott and Hart
> ORGANIZATIONAL AMERICA

So as our tenure in organizations continues, we come to accept and create, usually without contemplation, our own dispensability. By embracing the linear career strategy, we become overly specialized, losing our flexibility and freedom of choice. We become standardized, interchangeable parts in a huge corporate machine.

Loyalty

Organizations also require loyalty—loyalty that must come before our peers, friends, community, and even before our families. Organizations evaluate us by the degree of our adherence to its values more than by the quality of our work.

Uniformity

Whyte and others claim that the ultimate outcome of the organizational imperative is to impose uniformity on all who enter as a requisite condition of survival in an organizational culture. The organization man and the man in the gray flannel suit may have changed into more contemporary garb, but they're still with us. In the face of intensifying competition, we risk becoming serfs, indentured to our corporate, professional, or academic masters as a

tradeoff for the golden handcuffs of comfort and security.

Jeff's Story

I got into software development years ago when it was an infant field. I was in on the ground floor. I liked it because it had a future and because it was exciting. I felt like I was really doing something. I was promoted a number of times and finally made it into middle management, where I've been for eight years. And I hate to admit it, but I don't like my work anymore and haven't for a long time. It's pushing papers. Every day papers and reports. I love programming, but I rarely do it these days. The last couple of years, I've been spending a lot of time thinking that there are other things I'd rather do. I'd like to work with people, maybe in training or something like that. But I can't. If I try to transfer into that area, even within the company, I'll have to give up a big chunk of my pay and, of course, responsibility and just general clout. So I'm stuck here. I can't go out and find another job because, quite frankly, the truth of the matter is that I'm overpaid. I just don't see how I can get the same salary anywhere else. So I'm a prisoner in a plush cell. I'm wearing golden handcuffs.

> Note: At the time of this statement, the mortgage
> on the four-bedroom modern suburban home Jeff shared
> with his wife was under $1000 a month—much less
> than most of his colleagues were paying for rent. And
> their liquid assets were more than three times Jeff's
> annual salary. Jeff was blind to the fact that his nest
> egg did provide him with options. For example, he
> could have taken a position in a new field at half his
> current salary while maintaining his current life-style
> for more than six years. But instead, Jeff was inden-
> tured to his specialized linear career track.

Totalitarianism Evolves

Earl Shorris describes the totalitarian techniques
of organizations in *The Oppressed Middle: Politics of
Middle Management.* He says that most important
element in any totalitarian organization is the power
of the organization to assign or withdraw the means
of earning a living. Organizations don't set out to
be totalitarian. If they did, they would attract no
more than a few lunatics to their membership.
Totalitarianism evolves. We choose totalitarianism out
of fear, because it holds an end to suffering and
insecurity. In return it asks that we give nothing but
our autonomy.

University of Washington organization specialists
William Scott and David Hart point out, "The
benefits of the organizational imperative do not
come for free; everyone must pay. And paying the
debt has required us all to surrender our allegiance
to the traditional American values [of individual-
ism]." Such behavioral and value alterations are not
painful because we have created a society in which
those who are loyal to the organizational imperative
are amply rewarded.

Rule by Nobody

There is no one to picket against, boycott, or
appeal to. For even the leader of the organization is
a dispensable human part as we witnessed in the
mid-1990s with the firing of Steve Jobs, the founder
and CEO of Apple Computer.

From the chief executive office to the clerks and assemblers, we're all equally powerless. "We have tyranny without a tyrant. Bureaucracy has taken on a life of its own making society answer to a despot in the person of nobody, leaving us utterly helpless or hopeless without the possibility of appeal," Arendt explains.

Organizational bureaucracy or the rule of an intricate system of bureaus in which [no one] can be held responsible can properly be called Rule By Nobody. But Rule By Nobody is not no rule. Rule By Nobody is the most tyrannical of all, since there is no one who can even be asked to answer for what is being done.

—Hannah Arendt

Cited in THE OPPRESSED MIDDLE

Benevolent Tyranny

We trade autonomy for material benefits and the illusion of security. Whyte concurs, "It is not so much that the organization is going to push the individual around more than it used to. It is that it is becoming increasingly hard to figure out when we are being pushed around." It is easy to fight obvious tyranny but it is not easy to fight benevolence. Large organizations are not to be condemned out of hand. That is what makes the problem difficult as well as interesting. "Organizations serve us and rule us; increase our scope and hem us in," emphasizes social philosopher John Gardner.

The fault is not in the machine or in the pressures of Industrial Society; it lies in the stance we assume before these pressures and in the arrangement of functions that ignores our needs as individuals.

The organization is coercive to the extent that the individual has no alternative to a given course of action. Organizations make humans adapt to the machine, rather than the reverse. We must learn to make technology serve people not only in the end product but in the doing.

Nothing can be further from the values of self-fulfillment seekers, sometimes called "cultural creatives," than corporate feudalism—the hierarchical, authoritarian, adversary attitudes that characterize the organizational outlook in many American industries.

Chapter 4

Corporate Feudalism

Although we live in a modern and free society, our freedom continues to be curtailed by corporate feudalism which is a way of organizing work that diminishes the personal power of the people who work there. Corporate feudalism has three characteristics that limit individual power.

Standardization

The first way corporate feudalism limits our power is through the division of labor or the machine approach to designing and interfacing job functions. When jobs are standardized, people can be moved in and out of job slots like interchangeable parts in the organizational machine. Expected to act machine-like, workers learn to be cool and rational. Demonstrations of emotion or reliance on intuition are frowned upon as inappropriate.

An advantage of standardization to the company machine is that it need invest only minimally in employee development. Rather than training its staff, the company merely has to find the correctly fitting human part. If the part is scarce, headhunters are called upon to cannibalize the part from another corporate machine.

Specialization

Becoming a very special part is the optimal career strategy in such a system. By specializing, people can reduce their competition while increasing their market value. The secret of success in a feudal organization is selecting a winning career track by specializing in a high-demand profession or trade. Once selected, the track becomes a lifelong commitment.

With each promotion comes more responsibility, more money, and sometimes more discretion so that at first, power seems to increase with upward movement. But enhancement of personal power is an illusion. The longer a track is followed, the more restricting it becomes. Rather than open up opportunities, linear tracks limit movement options.

Even when workers move to another company, they rarely switch tracks. As in all feudal societies, there are rigid barriers between classes. Serfs could not become merchants nor could clergy become samurai. Similarly, under corporate feudalism, secretaries cannot become executives, nor can craftspeople become professionals. Career choices made early are binding.

Not having the mobility to shift career tracks creates the effect of being a vassal, the second characteristic of corporate feudalism. The indentured are not free to do as they please or to do the work of their choice. Instead, they are bound by obligations in which someone (or some entity) is the final arbitrator of their fate.

Loyality

The third characteristic of feudalism is the demand for absolute fealty. European feudal kings rewarded the loyal baron just as Japanese shogun rewarded the loyal daimyo with territorial domains or fiefs. These landlords, in return, rewarded loyal subjects, usually high-ranking knights or samurai, with stipends and small land grants. Similarly, under corporate feudalism, loyalty to The Company Way is more important than performance as a criterion for advancement and recognition. Performing in accordance with The Company Way is paramount even when there may be a better way. Those who are loyal to this standard are rewarded with promotions and increased responsibility domains.

Three of the outstanding characteristics of bureaucracy were permanence, hierarchy, and a division of labor. These characteristics molded the human beings who manned the organization.

Permanence—the recognition that the link between man and organization would endure through time—brought with it a commitment to the organization.... Longevity bred loyalty. In work organizations, this natural tendency was powerfully reinforced by the knowledge that termination of one's links with the organization often meant a loss of the means of economic survival.... To keep his job [the bureaucrat] willingly subordinated his own interests and convictions to those of the organization.

Power-laden hierarchies, through which authority flowed, wielded the whip by which the individual was held in line. Knowing that his relationship with the organization would be relatively permanent (or at least hoping that it would be) the organization man looked within for approval. Rewards and punishments came down the hierarchy to the individual so that the individual, habitually looking upward at the next rung of the hierarchical ladder, became conditioned to subservience.

Finally, the organization man needed to understand his place in the scheme of things; he occupied a well-defined niche, performed actions that were also well defined by the rules of the organization, and he was judged by the precision with which he followed the book. Faced by relatively routine problems, he was encouraged to seek routine answers. Unorthodoxy, creativity, venturesomeness were discouraged, for they interfered with the predictability required by the organization of its component parts.

—*Alvin Toffler*
FUTURE SHOCK

Having broken out of corporate feudalism, ronin do not exhibit fealty to The Company Way. Instead they focus on accomplishing project goals. When meeting goals means doing things differently from The Company Way, ronin find a route around the rules in search of excellence in completion of the project.

The Price of Security

Promise of security is the primary motivation for accepting the constraints of corporate feudalism. Peasants and knights alike were willing to be indentured because the lord, assuming he was a good one, protected them from roving bands and other outsiders. The lord did more than protect—he also provided. He established a market-

Corporate Feudalism

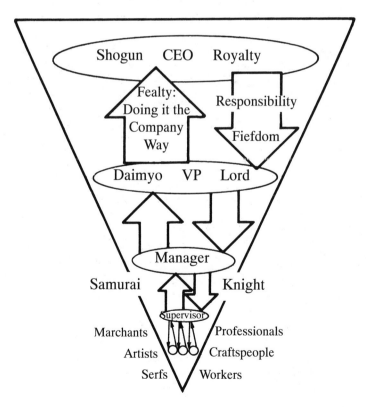

place and carried out judiciary functions, for example. Similarly, companies take care of health insurance, maintain credit unions, and so forth.

The hidden price for the security provided by corporate feudalism is diminished freedom and constricted personal power. Choices and mobility are limited, and corporate goals take precedence over both project and personal goals. Bureaucracies, like all feudal systems, are structured in tiers or a hierarchy that funnels power to the top. Royalty oversee the lords; the lords oversee the warriors; and the warriors preside over the serfs. This is the bureaucratic model.

We Were Beholden

The linear career strategy was a winner in the Postwar Growth Era, the heyday of Industrialism. But as we specialized, we became, without realizing it, interchangeable, standardized parts in the industrial machine, the organization. Jobs were defined, classified, and standardized. Just as an auto mechanic can order new plugs when the old ones misfire or replace worn wheel bearings, the organization can replace specialized workers.

At first, the rewards were high. Once on the track, you could expect to be carried along by the momentum. There was security in one's niche and a fat paycheck that increased periodically, bountiful luxuries and gadgets to buy, and a feeling of accomplishment as we worked our way up through the levels in the organizational chart toward the top. Few realize they were beholden. As long as the economy was booming and industry is growing, everything was roses—or so it seemed.

Specialization curtails freedom. Once on the track, we can't get off without going back to the starting place at square one. Job functions are narrow and routine. Continuity is disrupted, and rarely is one able to follow a project through from beginning to end. As the range of functions gets narrower, the worker's personality becomes lopsided. Self-actualization and the development of one's full potential are impossible. We become rigid, losing the ability to learn and adapt, and we become vulnerable to job burnout and the mid-life crisis.

Chapter 5

Vassals in Training

 The primary function of schools is to socialize youth to function well within society and its institutions. Gerth and Mills in *Character and Social Structure* say, "Education is a deliberate attempt to transmit skills and loyalties, as well as forms of inner cultivation and conventional deportment required by status group membership."

Scott and Hart in *Organizational America* agree: "The major responsibility for the development of the requisite character belongs to the educational system, and it has accepted this responsibility with enormous gusto, at all levels." In other words, most of us have been molded by schools to fit into corporate feudalism—the world of bureaucracies.

In his 1960s cynical underground dissertation, *The Student as Nigger*, Jerry Farber describes the socialization process we were subjected to and the demeaning ways we were treated in schools. He says: "For most of your school life, it doesn't make that much difference what subject you're taught. The real lesson is the method. The medium in school truly is the message. And the medium is, above all, coercive...throughout you're bullied into docility and submission." In short, education for conformity is more highly prized than is learning creativity or independent thought and action.

Educating for Conformity

Let's take a closer look. Each degree that we make it through indicates the extent of our socialization. With each level of advanced education, we are more finely socialized and thereby granted more power to play the World Game.

Admission to the World Game

Acquiring the first degree, the high school diploma, determines whether we are allowed to play the World Game or not. Those who do not earn a high school diploma are virtually excluded from positions of authority and power in our society, relegated instead to the lowest status and least skilled jobs. Yet high school dropouts, as a group, are not, as many think, less intelligent than those who graduate. In fact, according to Louis Bright, once Director of Research for the U.S. Office of Education, there is empirical evidence that high school dropouts, in large cities where figures are available, have higher IQs than do high school graduates!

> *Because of the steady increase of educational requirements for an increasing range of specialized occupations, the opportunities to climb the ladder of occupational success become more and more dependent upon education.*
>
> —Gerth and Mills
> CHARACTER AND SOCIAL STRUCTURE

Pushed Out

Often problems in school lie not in an inability to do the work, but in an inability to conform to the system. Rather than being stupid, high school dropouts are the "behavioral problems," who act in wrong ways or who say the wrong things.

Many students who show independence of thought are penalized with low or failing grades by teachers and are thereby restricted from participation in the World Game. For example, one creative boy attending a Catholic school heard a nun say: "You should love Jesus and hate the devil." He reasoned: "If everyone hates the devil, no wonder he is so bad and evil. I will love the devil, instead." Foolishly, he shared this creative notion with his teacher, for which he was given a failing grade and labeled a bad boy.

The fact is it doesn't take twelve years to learn what is taught at the secondary level. Recall Ferber's contention that *how* we are taught is more important than *what* we are taught. During secondary education, students learn to stand in line, sit quietly in their desks, raise their hands to speak respectfully to the teachers, and sit in study hall on beautiful days when they might rather be out having adventures. Students learn that to pass to the next grade they must have the right attitude and not notice when the emperor is wearing no clothes.

The high school diploma indicates that the graduate successfully made it through the secondary system—has accepted authority and can abide by it, at least to a minimum. Those who fail to conform are not granted the degree and are excluded from the World Game.

Trainee

Next comes the bachelor's degree. What is required to obtain a BA? Students, typically living away from home, are free of the constant parental overseer to prompt them to get up in the morning or to do homework. Instead they must prompt and otherwise manage themselves.

The BA degree indicates that a person has successfully made it through four years of college, with five courses a semester or

START

quarter. This entails attending each class under one's own direction, feeding back on tests and in class discussions what was transmitted in lectures and books, studying rather than playing on evenings and weekends, writing laborious papers, and memorizing innumerable facts of questionable usefulness.

It is no wonder that the new college graduate is prime candidate for management trainee! Holding a BA degree indicates one is malleable, trainable and can follow directions on one's own—without a mommy.

Professional

Next comes the master's degree. In many ways, this is the easiest degree to obtain. The course of study is shorter—nine to eighteen months—and in an area of the student's interest and ability. Most masters level study is in a "program" run by a team of instructors, who are likely to take each other's academic demands on the students into consideration since they know what assignments the others are giving, as compared to the mammoth loads carried by undergraduates whose

> I emerged from school to discover I was empty of enthusiasm. I had a profession but nothing to profess, knowledge but no wisdom, ideas but few feelings, rich in technique but poor in convictions: I'd gotten an education but lost an identity.
>
> —Sam Keen

every professor piles on long reading lists and lengthy papers. At the undergraduate level the classes are in widely differing subjects like Latin, math, literature, and biology as examples; whereas at the masters level classes interlock so that material from one assignment augments what is presented in other classes, which additionally lightens the load.

Upon graduation with a master's degree, one is anointed with the label "professional" and allowed a larger measure of respect, freedom and power in the World Game. Freed from punching the time clock, there is usually a substantial increase in earning potential and more latitude in one's work and greater respect.

Expert

The final degree is the doctorate. The first two years of doctoral training are perhaps the easiest of all the years spent in post-high school education. By this time, students are skilled at studying and able to quickly extract vital information from lectures and texts. They can "read" the professor to know what to feedback to get the best grade. They have the intellectual capabilities to analyze ideas and the writing and speaking skills to communicate them. They know how to get the grades and how to impress the professors.

The critical test comes with the dissertation. Up to this point, the student followed the authority of teachers, feeding back what they said, studying what they assigned, taking required courses, and meeting the teacher-set deadlines. But with the dissertation, all the rules change. No longer can the student rely on teachers for direction, structure, or feedback.

To pass the test of the dissertation, the candidate must do two things. The first requirement is successfully completing an "original" scholarly study or research project. This is the easy part. By the time doctoral candidates have gotten to this point, they are thoroughly acquainted with their fields. Thinking of something no one has done before is easy. More difficult is deciding which of the many possibilities to choose.

The second and critical challenge of the dissertation is that the student must do the original work—independently! Gone are the deadlines of tests and papers assigned by teachers. Students can literally go for months, even years, floundering around, not knowing how to proceed, making little progress. No one prompts, no one threatens, and few encourage the candidate to work.

There is no structure and little external support. After 18 or more years of being directed by teachers, students must find self-direction and create their own structure. Although the work must be original, at the same time it must adhere to rigorous parameters of intellectual discourse or research design. Many are unable to climb this glass mountain and drop out with what is commonly called the "ABD degree"—All But Dissertation—and are awarded a master's degree as a sort of consolation prize.

Conformity Internalized

Completion of the dissertation and the subsequent awarding of this highest degree indicate that acceptable behavior and values have been internalized to the extent that the doctoral graduates *impose them on themselves.* What is the reward for this feat of socialization? The label "expert" and, as a college teacher or researcher, being allowed to pursue one's work independently, with little or no supervision.

Although many believe that the Ph.D. is highly creative, even brilliant, this is often not the case. At every step along the educational process, those who venture outside of acceptable parameters of thought are given failing marks and not allowed to pass to the next step.

Those who survive the rigors and constraints of our present linear system are not necessarily the best and the brightest, but rather those who have become most wily in the art of bureaucratic survival—careful not to be overly creative and bright, more concerned with appearance than substance, never rocking the boat.

—John Oliver Wilson

AFTER INFLUENCE

Coloring outside the lines is bad—innovative thought is not safe. The highly creative are precluded from having too much power in the World Game. Only those who are safe, who are appropriately socialized are given enough power to push the frontiers forward.

Fortunately, schools have not functioned perfectly. A few innovative thinkers do succeed in sneaking through the labyrinth. These are the ronin. Knowing when to conform and when to be innovative, when to speak out and when to maintain a low profile, like Bilbo Baggins, they sneak into the dragon's lair and steal the jewels without being devoured by the sleeping dragon. For within the ivory towers of our educational institutions lie the keys to the knowledge, intellectual discipline, and technical skill needed to play the World Game. The trick is to obtain these while retaining a sense of one's self and keeping one's creativity in tact.

Educating for Change

Organizations find creativity and idiosyncratic behavior threatening. It's disruptive. Acceptance in organizations requires conformity and loyalty, and doesn't allow questioning or doing things in new ways. Until recently our schools have functioned well in shaping the people needed to fit into our feudal bureaucracies.

This process functioned to bring about industrialization and our modern world, but things are changing. It's a new Wild West—with new rules. The future requires more autonomous and self-directed people.

Education no longer guarantees a sure route to economic security and social status. The pyramid is shrinking. The economy swings wildly. Technological is changing our lives. We must break out of our narrow and rigid career patterns. Rather than following a linear career path, we need to be more flexible. When blocked in an existing job because there's no place for advancement, we need to be able to move laterally.

To do this, we must be generalists with more latitude in our career choices. Yet, schools still prepare millions of young people for corporate feudalism—to climb an occupational ladder that narrows dramatically at the top, thus ensuring rising frustration and increasing disaffection.

Educating for Autonomy

John Oliver Wilson in *After Affluence* offers advice for the education of flexible and autonomous people. He says that education should include programs in three major areas: basic skills, flexibility and alternatives and wonder. The course in basic skills should provide tools to earn a living. These would include both technical skills, such as accounting, engineering, or management, and basic communication skills of reading, writing, and speaking.

The primary aim should not be to prepare for a single vocation, but to equip the graduate for many careers. Whereas technical skills can quickly become obsolete, basic communication and self-management skills provide the flexibility needed for the world of the future.

Expect Change

A course in flexibility and alternatives should teach how to live in the world of change. Familiarity with alternative lifestyles and experience work in radically different jobs is essential. Wilson believes we must learn to create whole lives from our many varied experiences.

Course in creating structure and self-leading are both essential if one is going to move into the unknown. Wilson suggests a course in wonder to prepare graduates to develop what he calls "our inner silence, to cultivate the ability to let things happens, to welcome, to listen, to allow." I would add training in creating meaning which is vital for sustaining enthusiasm.

Financial Literacy

Feudal corporations need a steady supply of people to work in their jobs that traditionally have been mundane and repetitive. Most people stay because they "need the money"—a modern version of being indentured. Indenture is a contract by which a person is bound to service. This is exactly what an employee contact is—it obligates us to serve the employer to obtain the means to live. If we are bored or stressed out, we must stay on nonetheless because we have few alternatives.

> If you work for money, you give up its power to your employer. If your money works for you, you keep and control its power.
>
> —Robert Kiyosaki
> RICH DAD POOR DAD

We make huge incomes, yet most of us can hardly cover the bills. Suze Orman, author of *The Courage to Be Rich*, tells us that it's the interest—credit card interest, home mortgage interest, and car payment interest—amounting to thousands of dollars a year—that keeps us in shackles, that keeps us indentured.

The problem is one of financial literacy. A vicious cycle of "buy now, pay later" keeps us locked in. Financial ignorance keeps us indentured as employees, while financial independence brings alternatives. The indentured go from one paycheck to the next with few alternatives. ·We've not been taught how money works or how to make it work for us. Instead, we've been duped into working for money.

We've been brainwashed to disdain the subject of money as boring and discussing it in polite company as tacky. Ironically, the higher we climbed the educational ladder, the more we assume this paralyzing attitude toward creating wealth. It's hardly a coincidence that the stereo-typic college professor drives an old Volvo station wagon—presumably showing that love of learning prevails over love of money.

Neither a high education nor a large income is re-quired to become financially independent. The greater our passive income—income derived from sources other than from our labor—the greater our financial independence and the less we are forced to work *for* money. Yes, we all need money but our choices increase as money comes in independently of our labor.

That wealth and financial freedom come by climbing the corporate ladder and accumulating pay raises is a myth. What matters is how one manages the money one has. The financially literate make money work for them, instead of working *for* it. When your money works for you to create more money, you are freed to do more of what you want such as creative work that is not immediately—or ever—financially renumerating, or volunteering to help those in need, for example.

Chapter 6

Powerlessness

 A sense of power, the belief that we can influence the world around us, is essential for healthy functioning. Yet, we work in organizations structured to limit our power because powerful individuals threaten organizations.

When ability to control our circumstances is restricted, we are vulnerable. Threatened like this, "fight-flight" kicks in. Staying in the vulnerable state, rather than fleeing or fighting causes chronic stress which impacts negatively on our health and well being.

Consider This Study

Zaleznik and two other researchers from Harvard Graduate Business School surveyed the degree of stress experienced by 2,000 people working in three fields—staff, management, and operations—they found that there was no difference among the groups in levels of stress they experienced. They were all struggling with high stress levels.

It is commonly believed that there is a one-to-one relationship between stress level and stress-related disorders—that low stress levels go with low frequencies of stress-related disorders and high levels go with high frequencies. To test this Zalnick's team compared stress level data with the number of stress-related disorders—such as time off the job, drug abuse, and marital problems—experienced by each group. Because the three groups were experiencing the same levels of stress, it was expected that the groups would have the same number of stress-related problems. But the Harvard data did not confirm this popular assumption. Instead, one group had more stress-related disorders, and one group had fewer. Can you guess which group was high and which group was low? Stop and consider this for a moment. What is the reasoning behind your guess?

Operations Hit Hardest

Operations had the highest frequency of stress-related problems, and management had the least! The Harvard researchers found that the distinguishing variable between the two groups was the degree of power or control over one's work. Operations workers indicated that they felt powerless. In their work, there are few markers indicating completion of a project, for example. Instead, there is a continuous flow of work, with stiff output standards making it easy for anyone to see the degree to which they accomplished their production quota. Simultaneously they reported organizational conditions sabotaged their ability to produce those numbers. For example, operations workers complained that their supervisors were technically ignorant and that they couldn't communicate with them. Managers, on the other hand, have at least an illusion of control. The Harvard group hypothesized that it was feelings of personal power that buffered the managers from the effects of stress.

> *Bureaucratic practices set limits to the assertion of power by individuals in the organization, but the possession of power in organizations reduces the harmful consequences of bureaucracy to the individual. Therefore, survival in bureaucracies falls to those individuals who know how to negotiate a double bind situation while advancement in bureaucracies falls to those individuals who can make an opportunity out of a paradox.*
> *— Zaleznik, de Vries & Howard*
> *"STRESS REACTIONS IN ORGANIZATIONS"*
> *BEHAVIORAL SCIENCE*

In discussing their results, the Harvard researchers imply that feudal organizations severely limit feelings of personal power rendering them toxic to the human spirit.

Paradox

Feudal organizations thrust all who work within them into unavoidable paradoxes. Individuals create organizations. Yet once created, organizations develop an anti-individual consciousness. Individuals are a threat, and organizations act in subtle ways to eliminate those who exhibit individuality and personal power. And this often includes the very people who birthed the organization in the first place. For example, Steve Jobs, the legendary founder of Apple Computer, was fired by John Scully, who Jobs himself had hired to run the company.

Paradox

Individuals	Organizations
are:	demand:
✧ Ambiguous	✧ Clarity
✧ Unpredictable	✧ Predictability
✧ Imperfect	✧ Perfections
✧ Unique	✧ Standardization
✧ Emotional	✧ Reason
✧ Subjective	✧ Analysis

As organizations grow stronger, they focus increasingly on self-preservation. Clients and customers are tolerated as necessary nuisances. Common are stories of social agencies, for example, that neglect—and in some cases even injure—the very people they exist to serve. The mental institution in Ken Kesey's *One Flew over the Cuckoo's Nest* is a classic example. One could argue that the renegade, McMurphy, was the only mentally healthy person on Nurse Ratchet's ward. Certainly he was the only one with spirit and he inspired the others—that was the problem. McMurphy enlivened people.

McMurphy shook the patients out of their apathy and admonished them, by example, to assert their personal power. In the process they came to life with renewed enthusiasm for living. McMurphy inspired hope in the patients and fear in the staff. A catatonic Indian spoke for the first time in over a decade—a therapeutic breakthrough!

McMurphy's influence actualized all that mental health authorities profess is good for mental patients. Yet, his spiritedness upset the ward's routine. No longer were the patients docile; they were unpredictable. Nurse Ratchet's fiefdom was under siege. Rallying all her forces, she had McMurphy lobotomized—de-spirited. Or so she thought. For so strong was his spirit that it lived on in the patents' memories. Even after McMurphy died, they refused to believe he was dead.

Innovators Pushed Out

Peters and Waterman chronicle the cuckoo's-nest dynamic in corporate America in their groundbreaking book, *In Search of Excellence*. Those who act too individualistic, or who challenge organizational routines, no matter how outmoded or cumbersome, are pushed out. Those ronin who remain are continually blocked or moved into sidetracks. Never mind that the organization needs ronin to remain dynamic, innovative, and flexible. They are considered disruptive and challenging and must be neutralized. Allegiance to The Company Way is imperative.

Job Burnout

Corporate feudalism has an adverse effect upon motivation and productivity. Territorial domains are granted for demonstrations of allegiance to The Company Way rather than for excellent performance. Hierarchical control limits personal control and ability to accomplish assigned goals. The demand for fealty constricts freedom of movement, action, and thought. The loss of personal power sets the stage for job burnout, a syndrome that reached epidemic proportions in the late Twentieth Century and continues unabated today.

Job burnout refers to the depression and other symptoms that accompany the destruction of motivation and loss of spirit. Burnout is most dramatic when it occurs among high achievers, the front-runners, and the fast trackers. Once infused with enthusiasm, these high performers became increasingly frustrated and disillusioned. Steadily, motivation and productivity decline. As motivation wanes, we see disruptions in five areas of functioning: intellectual, emotional, social, physical, and spiritual.

Intellectual Disruption

Cognitive problems can occur at either end of the intellectual functioning continuum. At one end is boredom, an inability to pay attention or to become intellectually involved. Instead, thinking tends to wander to daydreams. At the other end of the continuum is hypervigilance caused by the high anxiety that accompanies burnout. Here thinking is scattered, moving erratically from one issue to another.

Emotional Disruption

Burnout is accompanied by increasingly intense negative emotions. At first, the contradictions and double binds of the feudal system engender feelings of frustration at not being able to accomplish assigned goals while being instructed to do so. Frustration ignites anger outbursts. Office rage is common. As performance drops and interpersonal problems increase, the burnout victim begins fearing job loss. With increasing insecurity, anger turns to anxiety. Eventually, anxiety gives way to depression and apathy as the person retires on the job. Often this progression is accompanied by alcohol and drug abuse, including abuse of prescription drugs.

Social Disruption

The demotivated worker becomes touchy. Small requests feel like unreasonable demands; minor irritants trigger emotional outbursts. Difficulty working with co-workers is the result. Increasingly, problems develop with spouse and children, often leading to separation and

Without work, all life goes rotten, but when work is soulless, life stifles and dies.

—Albert Camus

divorce. Withdrawal from friends and avoidance of social activities commonly happens as well.

Physical Problems

The burnout process is accompanied by a high degree of stress that impacts negatively on the body, making the person vulnerable to disease. At first, ailments are minor: gastrointestinal disorders, colds, and flu attacks, with a general feeling of being tired and run down. Later, ailments can be more serious.

Spiritual Dismay

There is a feeling of meaninglessness. "What is the point of doing this? I'm a rat on a wheel! Does this activity have any value? The hell with it all!" Such spiritual dismay is most dramatic in those making a lot of money and considered successful. Often they believe that if they make it to the next level, win a bigger fiefdom with respective increase in pay, then they'll have the promised life in the promised land.

When the thrill of promotion wears off, the new territorial domain rarely yields the promised satisfaction. After repeating this disappointing cycle several times, there comes a realization that it'll always be the same old grind and the person wonders, "Why bother?" A crisis of meaning sets in.

Working to Avoid

Corporate feudalism subtly encourages a "working to avoid" type of motivation. When territorial domains are granted on the basis of loyalty, there is an implicit threat that disloyalty or acting in any way that conflicts with The Company Way will meet with reprisal, possibly loss of one's rank and fiefdom. This engenders a subtle but pervasive fear of being demoted or fired. "If I step out of line, I'll be thrown out. I'll have no money. How will I maintain my lifestyle?" The corporate feudalist learns to work to avoid this free-floating sense of insecurity.

At each step in the hierarchy, feudal lords or organization managers are expected to keep all their charges in line and under control. Because the criterion for promotion is loyalty, not managerial ability, these lords tend to be poor managers. Rarely does the organization provide the training they need to assume managerial responsibility. Consequently, feudal managers tend to rely on punitive management techniques.

Punitive Management

Here's what happens. When productivity drops, a negative experience for managers who tend to resort to threats and criticism as a cure. In the face of these threats, their charges work harder and productivity increases. The result is a negative win for the boss, because criticizing employees helped to avoid reprisals from above. But rarely do the productivity increases last. When productivity drops again, the boss threatens and criticizes again. Quickly a vicious cycle of police-like monitoring develops.

Because the "working to avoid" syndrome is entrenched, corporate feudalists often get stuck. The control and threats to security become necessary to keep performing. Take away the threat, and they stop performing since they don't know how to "work for" positives, only how to avoid negatives.

Actually, training for "working to avoid" motivation begins in school. Students learn to sit in study hall looking busy to avoid the wrath of the monitors. They learn to stare at their books while daydreaming. They pretend to work while writing notes to friends three aisles over. If they protest this hypocrisy, they get detention and lowered grades. In this way, schools prepare students for corporate feudalism. Students learn a subservient posture.

Ronin, on the other hand, are more autonomous because they strive for more experience, opportunity, and skill rather than trying to hold on to their fiefs. Security for ronin is found in self-development—learning to be their own masters—to be self-directed warriors.

Chapter 7

No Peter Principle

The Peter Principle cynically states that people tend to rise in the organization to one level beyond their level of competence and then to remain there. This principle is frequently cited as the reason for organization inefficiencies and contradictions. The problem is that it tends to blame the victim.

Organizations take their best salespeople—as defined by The Company Way—and what do they do with them? Promote them to sales managers. The best engineers are promoted to project leaders; the best teachers become administrators; the best secretaries become office managers. But is managing the same as selling? As engineering? As typing? No, of course not.

Rarely is the promoted person given the training necessary to function successfully in a supervisory role. Instead new managers are expected to continue performing at an outstanding level at the same time as they are acquiring the sophisticated supervisory skills needed to do the job. Those who master this challenge are promoted again, and again, and again, until they reach the point where they can no longer figure out how to do the job while doing it. Cynics point to this casualty as an example of the Peter Principle.

Consider a question I frequently ask in my training sessions. Would you go to a dentist who had the same level of professional training as the average manager of your acquaintance? I suspect not! What does this mean? Does it mean that managing people at work is such an easily mastered, lightweight job that it requires little training? Does it means that managers are born with the skills intact? No, managers are inadequately trained which sets them up to perform poorly.

Managing is a Sophisticated Skill

When people are poorly managed, their motivation can be damaged, productivity drops, innovation dries up, and people suffer. What a waste of human resources! Think of any employee and try to calculate what it would cost, starting with a newborn baby, to "produce" that employee. It would be pretty costly! If an organization were installing a computer system of comparable value, inexperienced operators would never be expected to learn to use the system by trial and error. Yet, this is what they do with our most valuable resource—the human resource.

Managing people involves influencing what others do in a purposeful way. Substandard performance must be corrected, peak performance facilitated and maintained, conflicts mediated, participation encouraged, and so forth. In fact, there are many similarities between the behavior-change responsibilities of managers and those of counselors, social workers, and psychologists. A strong argument could be made that effecting behavior change at work is far more difficult than in a therapeutic setting. Professional helpers typically work one-on-one with clients for a limited time—usually a 50 minute hour—each week. Working with couples, families, or groups is considered vastly more difficult. In contrast, supervisors and managers work simultaneously with a variety of different personalities for long periods of time—40 hours a week—often under stressful conditions, while being expected to meet time deadlines, output quotas, and handle pressures from above.

Managers are Inadequately Trained

A strong argument can be made that managing people at work requires skills as sophisticated and complex as those of therapists and other specialized change agents.

Yet, whereas counselors and psychologists typically have extensive formal training and professional certification, most managers face these challenges with little or no training. For example, a social worker trainee is assigned one or more clients with whom to practice techniques learned in the classroom. Audio tapes and videotapes of the intern's sessions are reviewed with the clinical training supervisor. Similarly, doctors serve as interns in hospitals, and lawyers practice prosecuting and defending in mock court. In contrast, management trainees learn about the value of performance reviews, giving feedback, and setting goals but rarely practice under supervision or receive corrective feedback on performance. Even MBAs, who are schooled in the latest business theories, have little actual hands-on supervisory practice.

Poor Self-Management

Many people dampen their own motivation by managing themselves poorly. Perfectionists are good examples. Perfectionists set standards that are nearly impossible to achieve and consider themselves a failure if they don't perform at a near-perfect level.

Although they work hard, perfectionists get few wins and a lot of self-imposed losses because they act like a critical boss constantly berating themselves for imperfections. Working is not fun because it is fraught with frustration and failure. Besides setting unreasonable standards, perfectionists are stingy with self-acknowledgment and give themselves few rewards. Self-acknowledgment is central to self-starting and self-motivation, so it is not too surprising, perfectionists who negate themselves have difficulty starting and completing projects.

Vague Goals

Another important tool for getting started and maintaining momentum is goal setting. Poor self-managers set vague goals which makes it difficult to determine in what direction to move or what action to take. And when goals are vague, it is difficult to judge progress or accomplishment. Consequently, we can never be sure if or when we are winning.

Good self-managers break goals down into small, easily attainable, concrete steps. Poor self-managers demand that they accomplish everything all at once, in a few great big steps—which sets them up for frustration and failure—whereas the route to success is to move small step by small step.

Vicious Cycle

Poor management, whether self-imposed or coming from above, can diminish motivation. But worse, it can set a vicious cycle in motion. When we are poorly managed, our performance suffers. Drops in performance bring criticism and lowered self-esteem, which tends to adversely affect motivation. As motivation wanes, we tend to lower our sights and restrict our dreams—we strive less, achieve less, tackle less, learn less, and become less.

Innovation doesn't occur spontaneously in a vacuum. Power over our work—a feeling that we can make an impact—is an important catalyst. When we feel powerless, we plod along, performing adequately at best, but rarely innovate. A sense of ownership motivates us to invest the energy required to birth new ways of doing things. Corporate feudalism, work in which employees feel beholden to The Company Way—that they are powerless to influence—destroys motivation to perform excellently. To sustain high levels of motivation and promote innovation, we must feel we have the power to affect our work.

Empowering Employees

Empowerment is a sense of personal power, an I-can-do feeling, a sense that we can control our work. Companies empower employees by providing "good work"—work in which we feel we have an adequate measure of control—that we can accomplish our assignments, and that we are appreciated for what we accomplish. Work is "good" when it's translated into a goal that we can achieve and we participate in creating the targets. Further, good work is built upon timely feedback on our progress and acknowledgement for our performance.

Goals

Goals provide a target to shoot at. Goals provide something to aim for and help us to focus and to stretch our skills. A goal provides a beacon to sail toward—a direction—without which we can go around and around, getting nowhere. When we participate in setting goals, rather than having them laid upon us, we tend to set higher goals and to achieve them more often.

Participation

Research shows that when we participate in setting our project goals, we tend to set more rigorous ones and to achieve them more often than when we do not participate. Participation is a way for companies to tap into our abilities and insights about what we know best—our work, as well as a way for us to plug in.

Feedback

Goals are most effective when we get feedback on our progress towards achieving them. Without feedback, goals lead to frustration. Feedback is a major variable in learning because it tells us what we did that worked and what didn't work. Giving feedback is the corner stone of quality management. It enables us to improve our next move. Feedback is not just a rote "good job," but thoughtful comments on the quality of our work.

Acknowledgement

Attention is a potent motivator. It needn't be loud applause or gushing accolades. Well-timed positive attention for small improvements helps keep us going for the long haul.

Midlife Crisis

The notion that the midlife crisis is a virtually inescapable stage of male development is widely accepted. The belief is that beginning around age 40, men must confront unpleasant realities. Decline in physical and sexual prowess, mortality, the goal gap—the discrepancy between what he had hoped to do and what he has done—having to step aside so that younger men can step into the fast lane, and boredom are the most commonly cited triggers.

The finger of blame is pointed at the restrictive male role that limits men's acceptable range of activities and expression. What is overlooked is that the notion of acceptable male behavior has been defined largely by the needs of corporate feudalism. Men have been duped into becoming society's drones—the worker bees. By comparison, experts claim that women are much less likely to experience a crisis at midlife, and they handle it with less trauma when they do. This changes when women enter the executive suites and corporate boardrooms, however. Like men, corporate women work 80-hour weeks and instead of having a wife, they have nannies, cleaning ladies and personal home assistants.

> *Statistics show that only a handful of highly educated men will continue to move up the ladder after forty, while the majority will merely hold on to whatever rung they have already reached. And some, usually the least educated, will start to slip down. This is the reality in America . . . .*
>
> —Nancy Mayer
> THE MALE MID-LIFE CRISIS

The System, Not the Person

The feudal corporate system, with its straight-line track upward and specialization, is a setup for a crisis at midlife whether the person is male or female. By midlife, the worker is so invested in one direction that other alternatives, although not impossible to follow, require a tremendous sacrifice to do so. Worse, in the process of specializing, we develop only a small part of our abilities, which results in a skewed personality, with some aspects exaggerated while others lay dormant. Midlife is a time when many hope to move into middle management. And it is at middle management that the crunch comes, because the pyramid narrows rather dramatically. Add to this computerization of accounting and tracking functions, which make up a significant portion of the job. Many discover that they've been replaced by a machine—a white-collar robot—which works endlessly without a complaint—well, perhaps only a crash or a virus now and then!

Burnout in Disguise

People constantly use burnout and stress interchangeably. But the two are very different. Stress is a result of overtaxing our bio-system, which can lead to illness—a system breakdown. Burnout, which can be liken to job depression, is caused by feelings of powerlessness and loss of a sense of control and feeling unable to make an impact. Burnout dampens enthusiasm and diminishes motivation, which can lead to a system shutdown.

A stressed person can be beaming with enthusiasm and be highly motivated; whereas a person suffering burnout feels down, demotivated, demoralized and depressed, and finds it difficult to perform.

"Entho" is the root of enthusiasm and means "the god within." During burnout we lose touch with the god within. We are de-spirited. It is painful and difficult to reverse without that special spark from within.

Feeling unable to move up and unable to change, the linear strategist at midlife is a prime candidate for burnout—another casualty of corporate feudalism. What a waste of our precious human resource!

Mid-Life Flowering

People on the specialized inside track tend to be successful in the beginning, when they are young. Promotions come fast, as they move ahead quickly. By comparison, in the early stages, ronin often appear unfocused. Promotions are sacrificed for lateral and nonlinear moves, as ronin follow their interests rather than specializing. Ronin are often seen as making little progress because they believe that the quality of the journey is what is important, not making it to the next rung on the ladder.

But at midlife, ronin have an entirely different experience. Ronin are less likely than corporate feudalists to regret the paths not taken or to feel their lives lack meaning, challenge, or adventure. At midlife, those who have followed a linear track find that advancement slows, perhaps stops. This is doubly difficult for the fast trackers, who have come to expect rapid advancement and define their self-worth in these terms.

For ronin, on the other hand, midlife is a time of flowering because at midlife, ronin come into their own. A breadth of skills forged from a range of experiences is drawn upon in unique ways. Rather than feeling locked into an unfulfilling job, at midlife ronin experience success, often quite dramatic. It is a time of maximum influence, of being able to participate fully and creatively in the World Game.

PART TWO

EMERGING RONIN

Chapter 8

Free Agents

Out of the collision between the quest for more flexibility, self-fulfillment, and opportunity to develop our full potential and the wild economic swings, the increasingly rapid technological changes, the uncertainty, and the confusion is emerging a new breed of worker: the ronin. Who are ronin? We are everywhere, emerging in every industry and in every walk of life. Perhaps even you, yourself, are an emerging ronin.

Early in the feudal period surviving as a free agent in the rigidly structured Japanese society was nearly impossible. For one thing, *ronin* had no independent money so even meeting basic survival needs, like food and shelter, was a challenge. The end of Japanese feudal period in 1867 brought with it great social change. Traditionally indentured to a feudal lord or provincial army, many samurai who had been property and did as they were ordered, became *ronin* when the armies were disbanded. Unaffiliated samurai, those who were no longer indentured, were set free to fend for themselves.

History of Ronin

As early as the eighth century the word *ronin*, which translates literally as "wave-people," was used in Japan to describe people who left their allotted stations in life. Most commonly, it refers to samurai who left the service of their feudal lords to become masterless.

When a samurai was severed from his lord, he had two choices: to commit *seppuku*—ritual disembowelment—or to *do ronin*. If he chose to *do ronin*, he lost his stipend and forfeited all formal affiliations and duties, because no provisions were made in feudal Japanese society for those who were dislodged. Earning enough to survive was exceedingly difficult because feudal societies had no pay-for-service system, as we know it.

Being disavowed in a society build upon rigidly defined relationships was a challenge to develop self-directedness. Dislodged from their niches, *ronin* were considered thrown on the waves of a difficult and uncertain destiny. *Doing ronin* was accepted as a spiritual trial thrust upon one by misfortune or by the order of one's *bushi* master. Those who passed the test did so by following *bushido*—the way of the warrior, and by mastering *butjutsu*—the practice of martial arts.

Extreme Control

Under the rule of the Tokugawa dictatorship (1600-1867), citizens of feudal Japan were subjected to a stringent system of control. Farmers were registered in their villages and forbidden to leave. Merchants and artisans had to be registered with appropriate guilds and any activity considered irregular was reported to shogunate officials. Affiliated warriors were closely monitored through a chain of supervisors linked vertically by the institution of vassalage, which built upon a tight master-subordinate unit. Vassals were expected to exhibit unquestioning loyalty to the superior.

Control over movement in the cities was maintained through special gates installed across intersections of every two streets, with passes required of even the highest officials and their families. Penalties for unauthorized movement and other crimes were harsh and inflicted upon the entire family of the guilty party. Intolerance of anything that might have forced a person to confront individual values different from those of society made it extremely unlikely that anything unexpected would happen.

Domesticated Warriors

In a land made up of hundreds of competing fiefs, warriors were essential for more than four centuries. Eventually the Tokugawa dictatorship closed the borders, stamped out Christianity, and suppressed the incessant conflict. Without wars, the warriors' role changed as they were slowly domesticated by their many nonmilitary duties. By 1700, samurai—the affiliated warriors—had been surreptitiously turned into civil bureaucrats hidden beneath swords, military titles, court rituals, and a host of routine guard duties. This is when *ronin*, who continued to live by *bushido*, stood out most starkly and were regarded with suspicion—and awe. It is from this period that the ronin metaphor, as it is used here, is drawn.

It was such a difficult experience that unaffiliated samurai were called *ronin* or "waveman"—*ro* for wave, and *nin*, like *ninja*, for man—because the lone samurai was cast into chaotic and uncertain waves. Sometimes the *bushi* master ordered a samurai to *do ronin*—a difficult spiritual trial of surviving on one's own resources in an inhospitable world.

Ronin Archetype

The West has many historical parallels to the ronin archetype. The term *free lance* has it origins in the period after the crusades, when a large number of knights were separated from their lords. Like their Japanese counterparts, they had to use their skills and live by their wits and swords. "Renaissance man" refers to a multi-skilled cultured person, concerned with self-development and educated in both science and art. Similarly, *ronin* composed *haiku* poetry, arranged flowers, practiced calligraphy, and developed inner discipline in addition to wielding a sword.

America's Wild West was fertile ground for the ronin archetype. *Maverick,* derived from the Texan word for unbranded steer, is used to describe a free and self-directed individual. Paladin, who appeared in the famed 1960s television series, "Have Gun, Will Travel," was a hired gun who made a career out of adventure and embodies the archetype.

Leland Stanford is an example of an American frontier ronin. From humble origins and with only a limited formal education, he emerged to make millions in the development of the West. When his only son died unexpectedly, he founded a university in his honor. Leland Stanford Junior University has become one of the world's great universities, which spawned the booming Silicon Valley that is changing civilization as we know it.

Different Attitudes

Ronin look like other people. The difference is in attitude and life planning strategy. Ronin project an aura of autonomy, of being guided from within. They take command and direct their lives. Ronin do not seek security in one job, in one place, doing one thing. Ronin don't just react to change; they take the initiative and direct their lives. They surf the waves rather than being buffeted about by them.

Guided by the belief that change is the only constant, ronin develop skills, attitudes, and habits of mind that become adaptable instruments of continuous change and growth. Ronin do not exhibit fealty to organizations, but strive instead for excellence through accomplishing project goals, even if it means going against The Company Way, as it often does.

Like Paladin, the frontier gunslinger whose famed calling card read, "Have Gun, Will Travel," ronin use their skills, whether they be sword fighting, gunslinging, selling, doctoring, or teaching, as tickets to ride. For ronin, one's career is an adventure of self-realization—developing oneself to the fullest by encountering and overcoming challenges and risk.

Ronin Led the Transition

Ronin played a key role in Japan's abrupt and amazing transition from a feudal society to industrialism. Under feudal rule, warriors were not allowed to think freely or to act according to their own will. On the other hand, having been forced by circumstances to develop independence, *ronin* took more readily to new ideas and technology and became increasingly influential during the transition because they made up a substantial percentage of the faculty in the independent schools. These private schools, which taught science, mathematics, and commerce, were more liberal and than the official government schools, which taught only the traditional curriculum. Consequently, *ronin* were more acquainted with Western developments and the avant-garde.

Many were instrumental in chauffeuring in industrialism by founding great Japanese corporations. Traditionally, it was considered demeaning for samurai to be involved in mercantile activity—somewhat like our contemporary academic Ph.D.s. So only those who had broken out of the old beliefs attempted to develop astute business skills. A good example is Yataro Iwaski, who in 1870 founded Mitsubishi, three years after the overthrow of the Tokugawa rule which formally marked the end of feudalism. Well over a hundred years later Mitsubishi is still one of the world's greatest corporate empires, with revenues exceeding $65 billion in the later part of the 20th century.

Change Masters

Being able to change, ronin do not resist, but expect change instead and prepare for it by developing a broad base of expertise and skills. Ronin do not pay allegiance to any one career track or organization, instead they use their interests as a guide, following one, then another to become generalists with many specialties. Ronin can wear many hats—and often do—to bring their diverse skills together in creative and profitable ways.

So while the linear-track specialists lose the capacity to adapt, which is so essential in our changing world, ronin are able to reorient themselves when the economy takes a downswing putting them out of work or if technologies change making their specialties obsolete. They are ready to catch the wave when the economy surges and opportunities abound. Ronin have a basic confidence, a sense of potency or personal power. This is their security. Ronin believe they will be able to deal adequately with whatever might arise and will be able to earn the money they need.

> *Don Juan, the famed Yaqui Indian sorcerer who taught Carlos Castaneda the Way of the Warrior, warns: Does this path have a heart? If it does, the path is good; if it doesn't, it is of no use. Both paths lead nowhere; but one has a heart, the other doesn't. One makes for a joyful journey; as long as you follow it, you are one with it. The other will make you curse your life. One makes you strong; the other weakens you.*
>
> *—Carlos Castaneda*

Meaning

Ronin know that meaning is found in traveling on the path and not in reaching the destination. Consequently, when making career decisions they are less compromising than linear careerists, who often find themselves on paths with no heart. Ronin refuse heartless paths because they expect work to provide an experience of growth through challenge.

For ronin work is personal. We want a sense of contributing and belonging, and expect work to be energizing while serving as a vehicle of self-discovery, a way to test one's limits, as well as providing for the basic necessities of life along with delightful comforts. Although all these ingredients may not exist at any given point in time in the desired amounts and mixes, ronin use the disappointments and setbacks as lessons in the quest to realize their potential.

Expanding Opportunities

As ronin advance along their irregular career paths, gaining more experience and more expertise, options multiply. When blocked in an existing job with no place for advancement, ronin move laterally in any number of directions. Ronin are resistant to job burn-out and suffer less trauma and psychological setback when they are passed over for promotion or miss out on a desired job. Viewing life as a voyage of explora-tion, ronin welcome unexpected turns. Changes, even negative ones, are accepted as opportunities to conquer new challenges.

Inner Motivation

Ronin do not measure success by the rungs on the ladder or the digits on the paycheck. For like their ancient prototype, they are accountable to their own standards based on growth and realiza-tion. In contrast to linear careerists, espe-cially those on the fast track, who often pic-ture their accomplish-ments on a football-type scoreboard, ronin view their lives as a giant canvas upon which they, the artist, paint with each experi-ence.

*All a person can do in this life
is to gather around him
his integrity, his imagination,
and his individuality
—and with these
ever with him, out in front,
leap into the dance of experience.
Be your own master!
Be your own Jesus!
Be your own flying saucer!
Rescue yourself!
Be your own valentine!
Free the heart!*

—Tom Robbins
Even Cowgirls Get the Blues

Less Vulnerable

When working in organizations, ronin are not as vulnerable as linear specialists to organizational control because their sense of confidence and autonomy are vital buffers. Although ronin don't like layoffs, cut-backs, or being fired, they know they can survive them.

Autonomous

Do not assume ronin are nonconformists; rather they are autonomous in the sense that they know how to act appropriately and will do so, when it makes sense and does not violate their internal guidelines. Likewise, ronin are not rebels. Instead, they consider work a medium for self-realization, the barbells that develop the skill muscles.

Entrepreneural

Ronin view themselves, much like a vendor or independent contractor, as working for themselves *within* the company. Stated another way, they partner with their employers. Ronin integrate their personal goals with company goals. Although ronin like comforts and the good things that money can buy, obtaining these is not their primary motivator. Instead, they are propelled by the quest for self-development, expression, adventure and meaningfulness.

Evolving

Being their own masters, ronin are self-directed, using work as an opportunity to set high goals to create a challenge and also to learn. Rarely do they allow their jobs to become static; instead they tend to rework the job constantly in response to the needs of the company or marketplace.

Clayton's Story

A lot of people are surprised when they find out about my doctorate in psychopharmacology. They think it contradicts my publishing developmental books for kids, but for me, it seems like a natural progression.

When I was in school, I had a lot of problems choosing what I wanted to do. There were just too many things I enjoyed, and I resented having to pick one for the rest of my life. I was very much into science, chemistry in particular. At the same time, people and why they do things fascinated me. Education seemed like a way to have an impact on the society. And I dabbled a little in poetry and writing. As I said, I resented having to pick just one of these and give all the others up. I thought teaching psychopharmacology in the university would be a good way to combine the psychology, the education, and the chemistry and promised to provide some money, some credibility—in essence, the good life. So that's what I did. I got my degree and my first assistant professor job in an East Coast university. I taught and did research.

But I became disillusioned with the university. It was stifling in many ways. Psychopharmacology seemed to be my best ticket, and I quickly landed a job as a salesman with a pharmaceutical company. I was good at selling because I was good with people; I listened and all of that. It didn't take me long to learn just about everything there was to learn about selling drugs to doctors. So this time I used selling as my ticket, and I landed a job as marketing director of a big toy manufacturer. What did I know about toys? Nothing. But it didn't take me long to learn. It was fascinating because I saw the connection with kids and the power that toys have over them.

One thing led to another, and I started leading sales training classes. At the same time, I'd gotten interested in the human potential movement in psychology. I belonged to a growth group and went through a number of personal changes. And I wanted to integrate them into my work. So I left the toys and began leading self-development and growth workshops. It worked out perfectly because I was getting restless and wanted to travel. So I got into the lecture circuit, which took me all around the country. But before long, I decided I'd rather not be spending my weekends in a hotel. So I packaged some of my stuff and started selling it I got a number of big accounts with schools and businesses and expanded into a publishing house.

Now I have a substantial list of self-development books for children and adolescents. I'm interested in the adjusting person, not the adjusted person—that's static. I'm interested in teaching kids adaptive skills that will serve them their whole lives. I'm really proud of our books.

You know, when I left the university, people told me that I'd ruined my whole life, that I'd never get anywhere and that I'd always be poor. But they were wrong. I've had a hellava good time; I'm anything but poor and I think I'm doing something important—helping kids have quality lives.

Oh, I won't stay in publishing forever. One day, maybe soon, I'll sell the company and do something else. I don't know what it might be. Oh, I have been getting a yearning to get back into science, and I've started to develop an interest in some of the problems in the medical industry. There are a lot of them, you know. So my psychopharmacology degree combined with my training experience might be a perfect ticket into the medical world. Who knows?

Evolving Path

Clayton epitomizes the ronin style of fluid development as he follows his unique career which evolves in his search for meaningful accomplishment. He catches a wave, rides it until its power—for him—slows, then catches another. There are no radical changes, rather his career path is an evolution as he exercises one interest or skill set, which leads to another.

Chapter 9

Wave Man

 Change is inevitable. Something we know but tend to deny. No situation is permanent. Time moves on. People are born, grow up, become old, and eventually die. Jobs, even the most routine and seemingly fixed, are fluid and changing. When the pace of change was slow, stretching over generations, society and individuals were able to adapt slowly.

But change is no longer stretched over generations. Reflect for a moment on how things were when you were a child. Picture your telephone. It probably had a cord, and maybe even a dial. Picture your family car. What type of features did that car have? Certainly no electronic seats that maneuver to fit to your shape, for example. Remember propeller-powered airplanes? Spaceships have flown around Saturn and space shuttles are routinely launched and retrieved. Soon, perhaps, we'll be commuting to the moon. Sound like sci-fi? Well, much of what we now take for granted *was* sci-fi not long ago.

> *The word "ronin" means literally "wave-man." It implies that the unattached warrior was tossed helplessly upon the seas of cruel destiny. Roughly, this is comparable to looking on a tiger as a victim of his environment.*
>
> —*William Dale Jennings*
> THE RONIN

As computers proliferate and expand in capability, we are transiting from the Industrial to the Information Era. The pace of change is speeding up, and will continue to do so ever faster. Buckminster Fuller, Alvin Toffler, and other futurists have pointed out that technology advances exponentially—that the rate of change follows the law of acceleration. For example, Toffler claims there were more scientists alive in the 1970s than in all the previous years of recorded history added together. According to visionary philosopher Robert Anton Wilson, this means our generation will witness more scientific and technological breakthroughs than all previous generations combined!

Technology is transforming our lives at home and at work. As whole fields of endeavor become obsolete, sometimes overnight, new fields simultaneously emerge. There will be more opportunities and more changes. Will you be prepared? The fact is we are going to have to handle change whether we like it or not. We cannot escape it.

Ill Prepared

Most people are ill prepared for change, especially when it is constant or comes unexpectedly. We grew up expecting to find a comfortable niche in life—a cozy home in the suburbs, a lifelong mate, and a secure and successful career. We were told and believed that by focusing our interests and climbing onto the fast track, we'd live the good life.

To make the American Dream ours, all we had to do was to select a specialty, go to school, get good grades, work hard, and cleverly play corporate or professional politics. Our schools, our institutions, our mores prepared us for stability, not change. While the indicators have been apparent for a long time, it still comes as a shock when so much that is familiar becomes obsolete like the proverbial buggy whip

Out of this chaos is emerging a new breed of worker—ronin who have broken with the tradition of career feudalism. Guided by a personally defined code of adaptability, autonomy and excellence, ronin employ career strategies grounded in a premise of rapid change.

Tossed into the Waves

Severe restrictions were placed on Japanese *ronin*, forcing them into outlaw status. To survive, some became scholars, others hired themselves out as bodyguards to rich farmers, some banded together and terrorized the countryside, and a few started schools to illegally teach martial arts to people outside the warrior class. One such *ronin* was Miyamoto Musashi, an illustrious undefeated fighter who in 1645 wrote *Go Rin No Sho*, which was selling briskly in the United States in three editions in the latter part of the 20th Century under the title of *The Book of Five Rings*.

With Change Come Ronin

The ronin archetype is especially relevant in this time of transition from one era—Industrialism—to another—the Information Society. With change come chaos, uncertainty and confusion. And in times of change ronin emerge. Ronin can handle the ambiguity unavoidable during such in-between periods. Those who employ new strategies and new definitions of success will be the winners. The traditional approach to conceptualizing and planning careers which involved specializing and following a linear career strategy to move up the promotional ladder, is no longer optimal because it does not factor in the unexpected. The optimal career plan in a time of transition must take the fact of change into account.

Although many of ronin's roots, such as *bushido* are in the male culture, most career women are well acquainted with the *way* of the ronin. Career women have left traditional stations and battled their way into the recessed of the male-dominated workplace. Most women's careers are characterized by a multiplicity of experiences and back-and-forth moves between home, work, and school, causing them to confront the crisis of self-direction. Like the *ronin* who had no clan, professional women often feel excluded from the corporate cliques' and inside tracks, without ally or mentor.

Reasons for Doing Ronin

Reasons for *doing ronin* were numerous and varied. Children of masterless samurai who maintained their warrior status were born *ronin*. Changes in the master's or the clan's circumstances could force a samurai to *do ronin*. He might be dismissed from service or request dismissal to be free to embark upon a trial of self-development or an adventure that otherwise might have discredited or involved his former master.

Revered in legend, such as *The 47 Ronin*, are the tales of samurai who joined the ranks of *ronin* willingly in order to avenge themselves or their masters. Most frequently, a samurai became masterless through a stroke of misfortune as when his master lost in war and was executed or exiled or when his master's clan was disbanded by order of the *shogun*. The progressive elimination of clans that were considered dangerous by the Tokugawa dictatorship eventually increased the *ronin* population to over 400,000.

Have Sword, Will Travel

After the opening of Japan to the West, many samurai chose to become unaffiliated in order to serve the Western compounds and learn from the barbarians, later returning to their clans to share their newly acquired knowledge. In time, a number of these errant warriors came to prefer this more difficult but generally more exciting mode of existence, which taxed their wits and imagination and forced them to develop their potential more fully. They became addicted to a life of comparative freedom. *Ronin* traveled all over Japan, meeting and accepting challenges, often going out of their way to seek them.

Forced by necessity to be individuals, *ronin* had to rely almost entirely upon themselves and their martial skill. As such, they were prime targets for anyone seeking a duel, because slaying an unaffiliated samurai carried no threat of retribution from state or clan. Consequently, those *ronin* who did not continually hone extraordinary skills and discipline met with a speed demise.

Like the ancient counterpart, the ronin emerging today are breaking out of the bonds of the linear career track or the one-life-one-profession imperative to which so many of us are indentured, following instead irregular, nonlinear career paths.

Independent Approach

In contemporary Japanese usage, the word *ronin* refers to would-be students who have not yet passed the entrance exams for the university. Mistakenly, many assume that these *ronin* are a Japanese version of the "high school dropout." Actually, in this context, *doing ronin* refers to a time of independent study. Although most student prepare for the stiff entrance exams by attending institutionalized cram schools, similar to our prep schools, *ronin* have a more self-directed strategy in which they hire tutors to help them prepare for the exams.

It is preposterous to feel upset when you are offered to do ronin. Those people who served in the reign of Lord Katsushige never failed to say; "You cannot be real samurai until you do ronin several times. You must have seven falls and stand up eight times. Hyogo Narutomi, I hear, actually became a ronin seven times. You must understand yourself as a Dharma (self-righting) doll. A Lord ought to give leave to his samurais for ronin trial.

A samurai once said, "Samurai fear becoming ronin because it involves thousands of troubles and miseries. So they become very depressed when they are told to do ronin. But once you actually do ronin, you will find it is not as difficult as you expected; quite different from your fearful anticipation. I personally want to do ronin again.

—*Tsunetomo Yamamoto (1659-1719)*
BUSHIDO
THE WAY OF THE SAMURAI

Occasionally, these *ronin* choose to leave college to form corporations. Kazahiko Hashi, or "Kay" as he is commonly called, is an example of such a modern day ronin. Instead of completing his degree at Tokyo's Waseda University, he founded the successful Japan ASCII Corporation and later joined with Bill Gates, a ronin from Harvard who started Microsoft, which rapidly became the world's largest software company.

Time to Do Ronin

We must be prepared to do ronin because our futures are unpredictable. White collar robots and the Internet are changing the face of the workplace. Relationships between bosses and employees and the way people are managed at work are undergoing scrutiny and alteration. Technology is ushering in new specialties and rendering old ones obsolete. To prepare, we must become more flexible and develop a new work ethic, one that meets the needs of both the enterprise and the individual. And with this in hand we can leap into the adventure of the *Way of the Ronin*.

Chapter 10

Have Skills Will Travel

Paladin, the TV frontier gunfighter played by Richard Boone, is a ronin-type character widely known in America. Paladin's business card depicted a knight chess piece and carried the motto: "Have Gun, Will Travel," to inform prospective clients that his martial skills were available by contract. The knight, however denotes that Palladin was not a mere hired gun, but a sophisticated strategist. Like Palladin, ronin are strategic and use their skills as a ticket to ride.

Corporate feudalism encourages unidirectional travel—climbing the ladder up which increasingly leads to a dead end. Because there is less room at the top, talented and ambitious feudalists get stuck mid-level. In some cases, they are pushed down a step or knocked off the ladder altogether.

Ronin avoid ladders and tracks and instead use their skills to move around the World Game. Ronin look sideways for opportunity and adventure, not always up.

They move within an organizations from department to department, team to team, or even one job to another within the same office. They also may move to different job classifications as Clayton did, who we met in Chapter 9.

Ronin move by trading on their skills. Generic skills are the most marketable. Self-managing, self-knowing, creating meaning, building structure, deciding, transforming, and communicating are skills of adaptability—of readiness for change. These are the skills that ronin practice and refine. Self-mastery skills, an assets in any endeavor, are transferable, enabling you to move in any direction you choose.

Manage Thyself

The discipline of the Japanese samurai is legendary. Faced with life or death situations, the samurai operated deliberately, with a steel will, unswayed by distractions. For many of us, mention of discipline and self-control triggers images of denial, withholding, and coercion, and not too surprisingly, we resist. Actually, discipline equally involves giving yourself pleasures and setting yourself up to succeed. It is a process of self-management in which you are both manager and managee. Critical, threatening bosses can extract reluctant, resentful performances, but managers who employ a positive approach get consistent quality output. The same holds with managing ourselves.

> *Self reverence, self-knowledge, self-control, these three alone lead to sovereign power.*
> —Alfred Lord Tennyson

Managing thyself is requisite to pursuing excellence, surfing chaos and riding the waves of change. Luckily, self-management is a cluster of skills and habits that can be learned and perfected.

Know Thyself

As with managing others, effective self–management requires knowledge and skill. But most of us have acquired our self-managing skills informally, usually from parents, teachers, and friends. Few of us have had guided training and practice. Consequently, we often manage ourselves in ways that sabotage our interests or that we rebel against.

How do you motivate yourself—by striving for positives or by avoiding negatives? Clearly, motivation driven by gaining positives— seeking motivation—is most desirable, because avoidance motivation requires a threat to avoid to get moving.

> *Man ignorant of self, creates his own unhappiness. The world masters him, when he was born to master the world.*
> *—Paul Brunton*
> THE SECRET PATH

When we focus on positives we want to achieve, seeking motivation promotes self-starting and finishing.

Break Your Inertia

Poor self-managers sabotage themselves by demanding that they make enormous steps which are too much to do in one step and cause them to become discouraged. We climb the mountain small step by small step. The surest way to reach a goal is to break it into achievable small steps.

Consider this principle from physics: The law of inertia says a body at rest will tend to stay at rest and a body in motion will tend to stay in motion. Just as it requires a tremendous effort to overcome the inertia of a large rock to roll it. Once it moves it takes less effort to keep it moving. The same is true of yourself. In other words, moving yourself toward a goal requires a larger effort in the beginning to overcome your inertia

Take Small Steps

> *The first step is the hardest.*
> *—Marie De Vichy Charmond*

The easiest way to get yourself into motion is through small steps, each requiring you to move only a short distance or to do something easy to do. When you do so you've broken the inertia and are in motion. Accomplishing the first step brings a feeling of success. Success begets success. Good self-managers set themselves up to succeed by demanding only very small steps—just enough to keep in motion. Avoid the macho approach if demanding huge steps, of forcing yourself to strain through difficulty. Not only is the large step approach painful, it is a setup to fail. When your momentum slows or plateaus, this is a signal that a step is too large or too difficult. Divide it into smaller steps to get yourself going again. Always think: How can I get moving?   What one small thing can I do to get started?   Then do it!

Self-Acknowledgement

Focus on what you do well.   Positive attention provides the encouragement necessary to keep making the small steps. Poor self-managers tend to do just the opposite. They focus on their failures and criticize what they have done poorly. Self-criticism tends to set up a vicious cycle of avoidance, whereas self-acknowledgment promotes seeking motivation.

Self-acknowledgement, is similar to positive thinking but is more refined, going beyond "in every day and every way, I'm getting better and better." Instead, self-acknowledgement zeroes in on the specific ways we have performed well and comments favorably about it to ourselves—and others.

The ability to self-reward reduces dependence on others for acknowledgement which increases personal power. Autonomy increases as we master self-motivation in which we reward ourselves for completing small steps

Avoid Perfectionism

Perfectionists are among the poorest self-managers—and the most miserable. Contrary to popular opinion, they are not necessarily superior performers. In fact, overall their track record often falls short. The problem is that perfectionists set unrealistic criteria for success—nothing less than 99.9% is acceptable. The realist, on the other hand, sets a high, but achievable standard, such as 85-95%—B+ to A— for example.

Suppose both a perfectionist and a realist are preparing a customer presentation. Who is likely to make their presentation first? Probably the realist who sets an achievable standard. While the perfectionist labors away on refinement after refinement, the realist goes on to give the presentation to a second, perhaps a third customer,

Because perfectionists set unrealistically stringent standards, they continually experience failure. Realists, in contrast, win more often. Perfectionists tend to self criticize, because they consider anything less than 99.9% as inadequate. Realists, on the other hand, make realistic demands upon themselves. and applaud what they do well—which is most of what they do.

Self-Punishing

To perform, perfectionists use guilt and punitive techniques to coerce themselves to work—to avoid their own wrath. Because they make performing such a negative experience, perfectionists tend to avoid working and procrastinate until the latest possible time. They spend their lives caught in a vicious cycle of procrastination and self-flagellation. For these reasons, perfectionism is a self-management approach that diminishes motivation.

Realists set high but realistic standards and focus on what they do well, to provide a steady stream of self-acknowledgement that fuels motivation, leading to more success. Ninety percent is an A, after all. Think about this: If you do *everything* at 90%—or 85%, which is a B+—or even 80%, for that matter—you are doing *very well*, indeed! When you set your criteria at realistic levels, you get more done, achieve more success, and enjoy yourself more.

Create Structure

Most of us spend years in school which structured all of our time and everything we did. Teachers gave us assignments and paced us through material. But the new workplace increasingly requires us to literally *invent* our work. A large measure of inventing is creating structure and getting started.

Structure creates clarity, helps us to get started and to pace ourselves. As you master yourself, you will become more adept at structuring your work. You'll be increasingly able to handle free-flowing, vaguely defined projects—the creative work which requires setting long-range goals and short-term action objectives, then dividing each into small daily, even hourly steps.

Self-Leading

Handling creative work often means performing in a reward-recognition vacuum for long periods. To maintain enthusiasm, you must look inward for self-acknowledgement to fuel seeking motivation. Master this and you'll be a true ronin, able to live by your wits and will, independent of the good opinion of others. Chances are you will never want to return to the confines of clearly defined, closely monitored work life.

Chapter 11

Manage Stress

The word stress, as we know it, was first used by Hans Selye to refer to a cluster of physiological responses—increased heart rate and adrenaline level, muscle tension, quickening of breath— he called the "general adaptation syndrome." He called it a general syndrome because the same pattern of changes occurs in response to a wide variety of events.

Triggered by Threats

Stressful events have one thing in common—an element of threat. The physiological changes occurring during the stress response are in preparation either to fight the threat or flee from it.

The stress response is "adaptive" because it helps us to adapt, to survive. When we overcome or avoid the threat, we survive; if we fail to fight or to flee, dire consequences usually ensue.

It is not possible to eliminate all stress, nor is it desirable to attempt to do so. Selye emphasized that stress is a beneficial and essential life process, intimately involved in physical development and in learning.

When Heaven is
about to confer
a great office upon a man,
it first exercises his mind
with suffering,
and his sinews
and bones with toil;
it exposes him to poverty
and confounds all
his undertakings.
Then it is seen
if he is ready.

—Moshe

State of Readiness

The stress response is an all-stops-pulled state of readiness, preparing us to move quickly and forcefully. Problems occur, however, when we remain in this state of physiological arousal for too long—when we do not defeat or in get away from the threat or when there are an overwhelming number of threats—changes—to confront. Our bodies are not constructed to tolerate a state of readiness for long periods of time. Resources and defenses wear down, leading to detrimental health problems and psychological dysfunction.

The relationship between stress and performance is curvilinear, not linear. What the chart below illustrates is that when stress levels or tension is low, performance tends to be low as well. There is too little stimulation to be able to keep attention on what is at hand. This is commonly considered to be boredom, understimulation, or depression.

At high levels of stress, performance is also low, because stress impairs physical and intellectual functioning. This state is often experienced as spinning our wheels. High stress interferes with creative performance and is signaled by hyperactivity, forgetfulness, frequent mistakes, lack of concentration, and irritability.

Because of the complexity of the modern world and the difficulties we encounter at work, as well as the increasing pace of change in our lives, most of us experience chronic high stress.

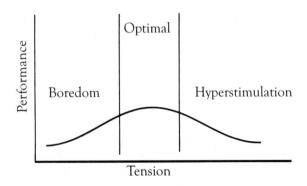

Stress: The General Adaptation Syndrome

Maintain Balance

The objective of stress management is to keep stress or tension levels within the optimal range for performance, health, and well being. That is, when bored or depressed, we should increase tension levels by listening to upbeat music, for example, or by taking a cold shower, jogging, working in peopled areas such as the cafeteria, or even by eating hot spicy foods—all of which are stimulating activities.

For most of us, however, the problem is being too tense and we can expect it to continue, as we must cope with increasing change. So it behooves you to know a number of ways to bring the stress level down into the optimal range.

It's a mistake to attempt to reduce stress by trying to avoid change. Although a natural tendency, avoidance is not acting in your best interest. If we are to grow

> A disciplined mind leads to happiness. An undisciplined mind leads to suffering.
> —The Dalai Lama
> THE ART OF HAPPINESS

and move forward as we navigate the limbo state between the old and the new, we must be able to tolerate a certain degree of stress. To move forward step by step, we must pick up the foot behind to swing it to the stepping stone ahead. Movement always supposes a letting go of the past position.

Stress Buffers

Stress buffers are situational factors that shield us from its toxic effects. Feeling that you are in control, relaxation, a strong social support group, and having fun buffer us from stress.

Prepare for Change

Feeling that you are in control—a sense of personal power—is the most potent stress buffer. It is the sense that we can influence what happens to us, which significantly reduces the detrimental consequences of stress. An effective method of increasing such feelings of power and control is to prepare for change.

Don Juan: Things don't change. You change your way of looking, that's all.... The world is such-and-such or so-and-so only because we tell ourselves that that is the way it is. If we stop telling ourselves the world is so-and-so, the world will stop being so-and-so.

—Carlos Castaneda
A Separate Reality

Consider All Possibilities

The most frightening aspect of change is the unknown. When we make the unknown known, much of the stress of change is dispelled.

The first step is gathering information. Find out as much as you can about the possibilities. What ideas do others have about what might happen and how to handle it? Talk to friends and associates; attend lectures; read periodicals, books, and newspapers.

The objective of initial research is not to terrify yourself with dire possibilities but to become aware of what might be, so that you can develop a contingency plan of action should a particular possibility come to pass.

Brainstorm Alternatives

Racing through the brainstorming stage, grabbing on to the first workable alternative that occurs to you, is a mistake. Instead, take time. The purpose of brainstorming is to generate alternatives—lots of them. List on a sheet of paper any and all ways of handling the situation under consideration.

Let your imagination flow. Don't analyze the alternatives when brainstorming. Just write down ways you might respond and things you might do. Include off-the-wall alternatives, which are probably unfeasible. This may prompt a breakthrough in your thinking that lead to creative, workable alternatives.

Try on Alternatives

Try out each alternative in your imagination, one by one. Play the scenario out to its conclusion in your mind's eye. Notice the pluses and minuses of the alternative. Notice new changes that the alternative sets into motion.

While watching the drama, be alert for pluses and minuses you hadn't anticipated before this viewing and for unexpected consequences of the alternative. How did you feel as you carried out the plan?

Finally, notice the impact upon important people in your life. You are not an island, you know. If you fail to consider and prepare for other people's reactions, a good plan can be sabotaged by those close to you.

Stress Inoculation

Once you settle on a particular plan, mentally rehearse it, which is an excellent way to practice. You can simultaneously inoculate yourself against the inevitable stress the change will cause, if it comes to pass, with the following simple exercise.

Again imagine the possible situation in your fantasy. Make sure to actively *project yourself into the scenario* so that you are a participant in the action. Engage all your senses—feel, hear, see, smell, even taste the experience. The more real the imaginary rehearsal, the more powerful the learning, and the more effective the inoculation.

Feel the Distress

This is important. For a few moments, allow yourself to *experience the anxiety, sense of loss, and other stressful emotions* that accompany the change, then imagine carrying out the proposed plan and see it working. That is, imagine events going your way—not dramatically, but realistically—and imagine people responding as you hope.

At this point, you will probably notice the anxiety and stress diminish because the plan provides a sense of control over what is happening. You are not helpless—you have a plan.

As Effective as Real Practice

Research has demonstrated that rehearsal of new behaviors in your imagination is as effective as actual physical rehearsal. By practicing in your imagination, you teach yourself what to do if confronted by that particular alternative.

Further, by allowing yourself to experience some of the accompanying distress, then seeing yourself handle it successfully, you actually "inoculate" yourself against the harmful consequences of stress. The process works much in the same way as a vaccination, which introduces a mild form of a disease in order to stimulate the body to build internal defenses.

Mental Rehearsal plus Inoculation

Mental rehearsal plus inoculation is an invaluable technique for handling daily life changes and crises. Anticipate the unexpected, experience the stress then practice alternative plans in your imagination. If you tend to worry, subdue the frightening images by creating a plan for handling them, then imagine your plan working. This will defuse the fear and strengthen you.

Relax

Relaxation is a powerful stress antidote. It is a regenerative process—a time of rest and refueling. Although it seems like the natural thing to do when tense, surprisingly few people know how to relax.

Breathe Deeply

When you are stressed, breathing tends to be rapid and shallow, which further increases tension. In contrast, slow deep breathing automatically relaxes you.

Even a few deep breaths will produce a noticeable change in your tension level. Deep breathing can be used anytime and any place. Several deep breaths just before a difficult situation are calming and increase feelings of control, for example.

Relax Muscles Directly

Another effective way to release stress is by alternately tensing and relaxing each muscle, one by one. You may have used this technique to go to sleep. If not, try it tonight.

Here's what to do. While lying in bed, first tense, and then relax each muscle. Begin with the toes, move up the legs, through the torso and shoulders; then tense and relax the hands and arms, and, finally, the neck and face muscles. When you finish, you will feel relaxed.

Used often, tensing and relaxing muscles has great benefits. For example, while doing the exercise, *dispassionately* observe the sensation in each muscle when it is tensed and then compare that sensation to how the muscle feels when it is relaxed. This comparison process develops your ability to discriminate between the two sensations, which helps you detect tension at an early stage. Tension-detection ability is important. Many people think they know when they are tense or relaxed. But the fact is we can be chronically tense without realizing it.

Build Community

A strong social support system is a stress buffer. The dynamics of how relationships impact on health are a mystery. Perhaps it is because family, friends, colleagues, and co-workers can provide encouragement, sympathetic ears, and feelings of acceptance and belonging. Mounting research indicates that people with strong social relationships tend to live longer, get sick less often, and report they are happier than those lacking satisfying relationships. Pets count, by the way. Research has shown that relationships with pets yield the same healthful benefits.

In a longitudinal study of doctors that began in 1946 when they were students, Caroline Thomas of Johns Hopkins University School of Medicine correlated extensive physical, demographic, and psychological data with the incidence of disease and death. Her results indicate that health and longevity are significantly higher among those respondents who have *stamina*. Stamina is resilience and the strength to withstand disease, fatigue, and hardship.

Thomas believed that an open, flexible approach to life; self-esteem; a spontaneous, outgoing temperament; and a minimum of tension, depression, anxiety, and anger while under stress are important elements in the development of stamina. The doctors with stamina in her study grew up in homes that provided emotional support, acceptance, understanding, and love. In fact, Thomas says, "bodily contact of all sorts is very important, especially hugs" in promoting health and stamina.

So make building and maintaining strong supportive relationships a priority. Not only do they feel good and provide a context for a full life, but also supportive relationships fortify against the stress of change.

Think Like a Warrior

Most of us would probably prefer to have a preponderance of positive emotions and pleasant sensations in our lives. Yet, all too often we succumb to a kind of thinking that creates anger, depression, and anxiety and, try as we may to think positively, negative, stress-producing thinking triumphs.

It is easy to believe that the cause of downer emotions is external, out there somewhere, caused by something somebody else did, or didn't do, when emotions are usually triggered by what we think about situations, the actual words in our minds and not the situation at all. How often do you hear yourself thinking, "He made me mad," for example? Another person cannot *make* you mad. Events do not *make* emotions occurr.

Don Juan: The most effective way to live is as a warrior. Worry and think before you make any decision, but once you make it, be on your way free from worries and thoughts; there will be a million other decisions still awaiting you. That's the warrior's way.

—Carlos Castaneda
A Separate Reality

What actually happens is that when an event occurs we *evaluate* it as positive or negative, good or bad, safe or threatening. Although we are constantly making such appraisals, we were largely unaware of them. Following is a classic example.

Sitting in front of a lovely fire, reading an enjoyable novel, you feel relaxed, comfortable and secure. Out of the corner of your eye, without being consciously aware that you are looking, you notice something move. Suddenly you leap several feet from the chair, filled with fear with your heart pounding. As you land, you realize that it was nothing more than a draft moving the window curtain, and you think,

"Oh, it was nothing." Seeing there is no danger, you calm down and return to the novel.

Undoubtedly, you have experienced a variation of this scenario. It demonstrates two things. First, our minds are constantly alert, checking out the environment for possible threats.

Second, outside of our conscious awareness we make rapid evaluations of events, the most basic being: "Is there a threat?" Anytime our minds determine that, yes indeed, there is a threat, the stress response instantly kicks in, mobilizing us to fight or flee. All of this occurs without any conscious thought.

> For the intellect is but a machine; it makes a splendid servant yet a bad master.
>
> —Paul Brunton
> THE SECRET PATH

We are appraising things all the time, and yet, we are largely unaware of it. We evaluate others' motives, too. For example, the head of a pharmaceuticals lab in one of my workshops described how his technicians often "capriciously" argued with his introducing new tests. He said it made him feel angry. I pointed out that "capricious" was *his* interpretation of their actions and not necessarily reflective of *their* motives. Perhaps their arguing resulted from the natural tendency of people to question and resist change.

Later this man reported that when he thought, "I should expect resistance to change," instead of, "They're playing with me and deliberately trying to sabotage my program," he no longer responded with anger. Instead, he saw that helping them to accept the new tests was a challenging part of his supervisory responsibility.

Chapter 12

Develop Your Zen Mind

Our biocomputers have two systems. One works with words, simple mathematics, and linear logic, using either /or categories and decision trees. The second controls creative leaps, music appreciation, and the formation of images. We also come with resident programs, two of which are safekeeping and discovery.

Safekeeping Program

The function of the safekeeping program is to protect and guard us. The famous psychology experiment with Little Albert provides an example of safekeeping in action. Little Albert, just a baby, was playing with a fuzzy white rabbit when a sudden loud noise frightened him, making him cry. The next time he saw the rabbit, he cried and refused to touch it because his safekeeping program associated the rabbit with the loud noise. Later, when little Albert met Santa Claus for the first time, he took one look at the big fuzzy white beard, began crying, and refused to sit on Santa's lap.

Safekeeping Program

Makes judgements, evaluates, trusts the known, identifies consequences, labels, seeks closure. Structures situation, creates rules, alert to threats, cautious, avoids surprises.

The Little Albert story demonstrates how the safe-keeping program creates categories to evaluate new experiences. Dangerous situations are identified and responded to on the basis of their *similarity* to other dangerous experiences. To Little Albert, Santa's beard and the bunny's white fur were lumped into the same category—white fuzzy hair that was associated with a loud frightening noise.

Inhibits Adaptation

The safekeeping program has much survival value, but it can be a liability in a rapidly changing world in which old categories no longer apply. Safekeeping programs protect us from dangers, but they can inhibit our adapting to dramatically new situations. And adapt is what we all must do now.

Discovery Program

The discovery program functions in a wholly different way. For one, it doesn't use words; it does not break things into categories or think in terms of either/or. The discovery program uses trial and error, which is essential for rapid learning and adaptation. If we are to adapt to the Information Era, which promises to change dramatically the very underpinnings of society, we must engage our discovery programs.

Practicing the oriental discipline, Zen, develops discovery capabilities. By developing a Zen mind, we are more able to handle change because we are less inclined to blindly follow the safe-keeping program while clinging to an obsolete past. Instead we become more open and receptive to a new future. The teaching and practices of Zen show how to bypass the ever-vigilant safekeeping program. But because the Zen mind comes from a part of us that is nonverbal, it is difficult to describe in words.

> **Discovery Program**
> *Imagines, feels, inductive, seeks novelty, sees patterns, is playful, accepts ambiguity, trial and error, experiments, pathfinding.*

Acceptance

The metaphor of the mirror conveys the basic elements of the Zen mind. The mirror teaches "acceptance" or "nonevaluation." When you step before a mirror, it reflects you without evaluating who you are or engaging a dialogue about it. A mirror simply reflects your image.

Unlike a mirror, we constantly evaluate everything, which is a safekeeping function that puts things into pre-established categories. As Joseph Chilton Pearce said, "We see through the prism of our categories." We do not respond to the "real" world at all, but to our preconceptions about it. Our reflections are like those of a funhouse mirror that distorts the image. This is another way that the safekeeping program undermines adaptability.

―――――――

Try this experiment.

Step 1: Look around the room for yellow objects. Do this now before reading on any further.

Step 2: Close your eye and picture the room in your mind. Keeping your eyes closes, in your imagination notice all the red objects in the room.

Step 3: Open your eyes and observe the room again.

―――――――

Unless you are remarkably observant or you peeked at Step 2, you probably had difficulty naming red objects. Because your attention was focused on yellow, you ignored things of other colors. You did not "see." A crucial first step in adapting creatively is to "see."

Let Go

When you step away from in front of the mirror, it stops reflecting your image. The mirror doesn't argue about it or cling onto your image. It doesn't accuse you of abuse and get depressed. The mirror simply lets you go.

Us humans are not as smart as the mirror is. When things change we often refuse to accept the new circumstances. Instead, we cling onto and demand that things remain as they have been. In so doing, we stress ourselves and impede our seeing and adapting to the new conditions. This is when our safekeeping program is most detrimental. When things change, we need to let go of the old expectations. We need to switch on our discovery program, accept the ambiguity of the moment, be playful, experiment, and find new pathways.

But if ever the least flicker of satisfaction showed on my face, the Master turned on me with unwonted fierceness. "What are you thinking of?" he would cry. "You know already you should not grieve over bad shots; learn now not to rejoice over the good ones. You must free yourself from the buffetings of pain and pleasure, and learn to rise above them in easy equanimity, to rejoice as though not you but another shot well."

—Eugene Herrigel
ZEN IN THE ART OF ARCHERY

Be a Witness

Mentally reviewing things from past situations with an eye to improving how we handle things in the future is one way we learn. But we often err in being judgmental and evaluating our performances, which leads to guilt and self-consciousness. When you use mental review it is vitally important to *suspend judgment*. Do not evaluate. Instead, sit back and witness—see the scenario. Let it unfold before you without making internal comments. Just see what is happening, like a mirror "sees." When you try this, you'll will find that it is difficult to suspend judgment. The safekeeping thinker persists in evaluating, putting things in categories of "good" and "bad". When this occurs, notice that you are judging and let the judgment go. Be a witness not a judge.

With practice you can be a witness in the moment, while performing. This is different from being self-conscious which is caused by negative evaluations of ourselves in the moment. Self-consciousness puts on the brakes.

Trying to be perfect, we fumble. The witness sees the fumble but does not judge it. The witness is you being aware of being alive now. The unfiltered awareness allows you to enjoy the moment fully and readies you for change.

Be Yielding

To be yielding does not mean to be passive, allowing yourself to be suppressed or walked upon. Instead, be like a blade of grass in the wind—bend when necessary, then spring back. Yielding means to be receptive, interacting with the world and responding to it rather than rigidly clinging to a particular position or posture.

When riding a wave, (the surfer) must strive to stay just slightly ahead of it, since if he moves out too far he will not be "with it;" he will lose contact with the power which has been propelling him along and quickly sink...if he allows the wave to overtake him, he will be overthrown or "wiped out" by the wave's crushing power, since, once again, he will not be "with it."

—Oscar Ratti
—Adele Westbrook
Secrets of the Samurai

Go with the Flow

Many incorrectly think that to go with the flow means fanciful undirected movement. Actually it means to find existing lines of movement and to go with them rather than against the movement. Martial arts employ this principle. By using judo, for example, a petite 95-pound woman can effortlessly flip a 200-pound man attempting to attack her. The woman does not grab and throw the man who is larger and stronger than she is. Instead, she yields to and uses his movement to propel him away from her.

Legend has it that the martial art jujitsu originated in China during a long cold winter. Each day, the snow fell on two trees in a field. Being firm and rigid, the limbs of the larger tree supported piles of snow.

Finally, the branches, no longer able to bear the weight of the heavy snow, cracked. The branches of the smaller tree also accumulated snow, but being supple, not rigid, they bent to the ground, letting the snow slide off, and then returned to their original positions. The tree that yielded survived the winter.

In our daily lives, at work or at home, to yield means to alter goals, as circumstances require. Like water flowing downstream, yield and flow around the rocks in life. Be flexible. Look for alternative and creative ways to reach your goals.

Accept Paradox

We tend to get trapped in either/or or dichotomous thinking. Yet life is not either/or; it is a continuous process. Because of the way we have been taught to think and perceive, we break the continuum into separate categories. But this is a false separation, an overlay of the rational mind—the safekeeping program in action. We judge ourselves as being good *or* bad when we are in fact, both good *and* bad. We struggle over emphasizing self-interest *or* the interest of others, when in fact, they are *both* important. We worry about living now *or* planning for the future, when we should live now *and* plan for the future.

> *We do not play the game of Black and White—the universal game of up/down, on/off, solid/space, and each/all. Instead we play the game of White versus Black. For, especially when rates of vibration are slow as with day and night or life and death, we are forced to be aware of the black negative aspect of the world. Then, not realizing the inseparability of the positive and negative poles of the rhythm, we are afraid Black may win the game. But the game "White must win" is no longer a game. It is a fight, a fight haunted by a sense of chronic frustration, because we are doing something as crazy as trying to keep the mountains and get rid of the valleys.*
>
> —Alan Watts
> THE BOOK
> ON TABOO AGAINST KNOWING WHO YOU ARE

Because of our propensity to categorize things into either/or boxes we are constantly confronted with confusing contradictions that immobilize us. Organizations, for example, are paradoxical. Organizations, which are made up of people, seek clarity, certainty, and objectivity. Yet people are not clear, certain or objective, they are changeable, and subjective. Believing that these contradictions should not exist creates frustration, confusion and attempts to conform to modes of being that are not possible to achieve. The organization with its chain of command is structured so that no one person has too much control or power, yet to be mentally healthy and productive, individuals must have a sense of personal power.

Shift Your Viewpoint

Problems that remain persistently insolvable should always be suspected as questions asked in the wrong way.

—Alan Watts
The Book
On the Taboo Against Knowing Who You Are

To break out of immobilizing paradoxes, we must look at the situation in a totally new way, making what Marilyn Ferguson in *The Aquarican Conspiracy* calls a "paradigm shift." We must ask the right questions. For example, people once believed the earth was flat. From that paradigm, intricate belief systems about the stars, moon, sun and their relationships to earth evolved. The discovery that the earth was round and circled the sun was a dramatic paradigm shift, one that altered the way of life. More recently, there has been another paradigm shift. For centuries, leading thinkers adhered to Newton's mechanical theory of the universe. But Einstein's theory of special relativity upset the basic premises of Newtonian physics, turning them inside out.

We are often unaware of our basic beliefs and guiding principles. A belief most of us have accepted is that the only way to success is to climb up the linear career ladder. Few people even realize that this is a career *strategy*; still fewer challenge it. Ronin have made a paradigm shift and do not unquestioningly accept specialization as the only career strategy and a straight-line progression as the only acceptable path to success.

When you develop and exercise your Zen mind, you enhance your ability to make paradigm shifts, to see things in more ways than one and to ask new questions. With a Zen mind, we realize that life and work follow both the principles of science and the principles of magic.

Laugh a Lot

Laughter is a stress buffer, but as with relaxation, the dynamics remain a mystery to medical science. Humor is a powerful tool for breaking out of paralyzing paradox, allowing us to look from a different vantage point to gain a new perspective and release tension.

When you catch yourself taking things too seriously, use this as a signal to laugh. Think of the "cosmic chuckle" and of the absurdity of our human condition. Satirize your dilemma. Imagine yourself in a Charlie Chaplain script. As a discipline, practice seeing humor in disaster. You'll find freedom there.

> Don Juan: Yesterday you believed the coyote talked to you. Any sorcerer who doesn't see would believe the same, but one who sees knows that to believe that is to be pinned in the realm of sorcerers. By the same token, not to believe that coyotes talk is to be pinned down in the realm of ordinary men. In order to see one must learn to look at the world in some other fashion, and the only other fashion I know is the way of the warrior."
>
> —Carlos Castaneda
> JOURNEY TO IXTLAN

The Donkey Chase: A Sufi Tale

Nasrudin, the playful teacher, was riding his donkey out of town when he passed one of his disciples who asked, "Where are you going?" Nasrudin simply grinned mischievously as he rode past.

Sure that the old man was up to something, the disciple jumped on his donkey and rode after him. When Nasrudin saw he was being followed, he urged the donkey on to trot. So the disciple kicked his donkey and chased after the old man.

Seeing that he was being chased Nasrudin took a shortcut across a field into the cemetery where he pulled his donkey to an abrupt stop, leaped off and hid behind a gravestone. On his heels, the disciple pulled his donkey to a stop ran over the gravestone, and looking over at his crouching teacher, he demanded, "Why were you running away?" To which Nasrudin asked, "Why were you chasing me?"

When you jump on your donkey in a knee-jerk response to chase after situations of the moment, you often create an amusing picture to those witnessing it. Always remember the cosmic chuckle and laugh loudly.

PART THREE
RONIN STRATEGIES

Chapter 13

New Game
New Strategies

 Most of us have been so indoctrinated into the notion of climbing the promotional ladder that we often aren't even aware that it's a strategy and that there are alternatives. In the Postwar Growth Era, following a linear path was a winning one. The economy and companies everywhere were booming and expanding. There was plenty of room at the top. All an aspiring careerist needed to do was to get in on the ground floor and find a winning track to ride up the hierarchy. Promotions and pay raises came quickly and easily.

Changes

Industrialization has ended and we are transitioning into the Information Era. Today, the linear strategy is perilous, filled with cul-de-sacs. The bulging number of baby boomers entering midlife and midmanagement are facing a squeeze. No longer is there plenty of room at the top. Instead, a majority of these eager, highly trained, and ambitious careerists risk becoming underemployed, blocked, even denied all while opportunities abound in free agenting, so-called dot.coms and start-ups. Many younger careerists are still relying on the same old climb-the-ladder strategy when the game board has changed.

Economic uncertainty compounds the problem. During periods of uncertainty, organizations respond by tightening up, becoming more centralized, and demanding conformity from employees.

Adding to these problems is the increasing speed of technological advancement. Many are trying to surf in the Information Era with obsolete skills, unable to know how to start or how to climb the corporate ladder.

. Future shock is here. In the midst of increasing change, many motivated and talented specialists are being disintermediated—replaced by white-collar robots—facing reduced options and feeling trapped. Unable to adapt,

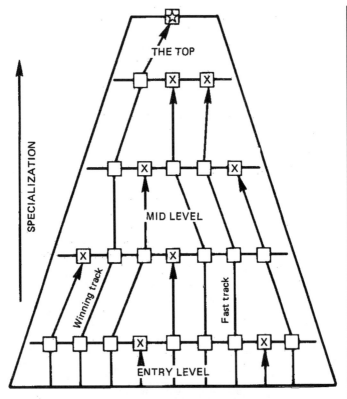

LINEAR STRATEGY
THE CORPORATE LADDER

many become victims of job burnout and the midlife crisis. Yet, at the same time, those who embrace change—the techies, the gen-xers, the entrepreneurs—take to chaos surfing like they did to their skateboards. Like fly-by-night operations—and almost as fast—they launch start-ups, turn them into IPOs ready to "flip" for a few million.

New Breed

From every corner of the nation, in every field, ronin are emerging out of this chaos and uncertainty. They do not subscribe to the traditional linear track game plan. Instead, ronin follow a new game plan, one optimal in the dawn of the 21st Century, a strategy that opens rather than closes opportunities, that allows for the development of one's whole personality and the pursuit of self-fulfillment. Ronin strategies foster adaptability, individuality, creativity, and diversity

Gregory Bateson—A Ronin

Gregory Bateson, one the greatest thinkers of our time, leaped into the World Game when he went to New Guinea to do fieldwork in anthropology. In the years that followed, he married and divorced Margaret Mead and zigzagged in and out of several disciplines—anthropology, genetics, biology, and psychiatry. He was, for example, a professor of anthropology at Harvard; he worked with dolphins at the Oceanographic Institute in Hawaii; he was a research associate at Langley Porter Neuropsychiatric Institute. As Bateson moved across disciplines, he left significant contributions in his wake. To psychiatry, for example, Bateson contributed the double-blind theory of schizophrenia and is considered one of the fathers of family therapy. Conjoint family therapy and neurolinguistic programming trace their lineage back to Bateson's work.

One secret to Bateson's creativity is that he applied patterns he observed in one area to the endeavors in other areas. For example, while struggling with questions regarding the arrangement of facilities and functions in a New Guinea village, Bateson remembered a biological organizational pattern he'd studied in the claw of a crab and suddenly realized that this biological pattern was useful in understanding village patterns.

New Game Board

For an alternative, we'll use the ancient Chinese game *Wei Chi*, or *Go*, It is played by placing stones on a board covered with many small squares. Like chess, Go is a game of strategy, only more complex and challenging.

The object of Go is to capture the most territory. Territory is captured by surrounding it with "stones" laid on the board in particular ways. Gaining control over territory and expanding one's sphere of influence is also an unstated goal in the workplace. The player who controls the most territory wins.

The Book of Changes (I Ching) *is often considered the Oriental apotheosis of adaptation, of flexibility.... The theme of this work is that everything in existence can be a source of conflict, of danger,..if confronted directly at the point of its maximum strength.... By the same token, every occurrence can be dealt with by approaching it from the right angle and in the proper manner, that is, at its source, before it can develop full power, or from the sides, (the vulnerable "flanks of the tiger"). If by chance, the frontal impact of events should over take a man, the I Ching advises him to avoid any direct opposition and adopt an attitude of " riding along" or "flowing" with the tide of events (a boxer might say "rolling with the punches"), thus keeping slightly ahead of or on top of that massive force which like any other concentrated force in creation, will inevitably exhaust itself once its concentration has been dissipated.*

—Oscar Ratti
—Adele Westbrook
SECRETS OF THE SAMURAI

Chapter 14

STRATEGY
Move Indirectly

The objective of the game of Go, as well as in the workplace game, is to control or influence the most territory by the end of the game. In the illustration Black uses a linear strategy as step by step, he places his stones in a straight line, with the objective of surrounding the area in the upper right corner. White, on the other hand, uses a nonlinear strategy as she proceeds indirectly towards her goal. Early in the game her moves seem disconnected as she places stones in divergent positions.

If the players continue with their respective strategies, whom would you bet upon to win this game? In all probability, White will win because it takes only a few stones to establish a powerful influence in a territory. While Black will definitely dominate the target corner, White will control several territories.

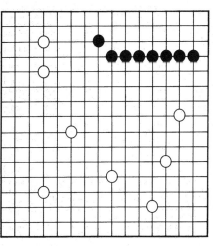

Go Gameboard
Nonlinear Strategy

Black employs the strategy of specializing. Like Black, scientists often devote an entire career to a succession of replicative studies, exploring variations of a hypothesis or refinements of a model, systematically filling in each square or small corner of a body of knowledge. This strategy has reliable success to the degree that in time the scientist will probably acquire influence over the corner, which White is not likely to challenge. But Black's influence, although secure, is limited to the one corner. At the end of the game when points are tallied, Black will probably control fewer squares to get a lower score.

Move Sideways

Similarly, the aspiring executive who hopes to climb the corporate ladder, step by step, to the top is assured of several easy moves in the beginning, winning a limited degree of influence. But the executive is unlikely to get past the middle management moves, where he finds himself blocked in, unable to move anywhere. Ronin, on the other hand, bypass roadblocks by indirect moves—moving sideways, occasionally even backward.

Take the Frontage Road

The "frontage road" tactic is another way to conceptualize moving indirectly. Freeway traffic jams can be by passed by exiting from the freeway onto the frontage road, which follows along side. Ronin take the road less traveled and zip by while others inch along the backed up highway.

Likewise, many prefer to take the winding country roads rather than taking direct four lane highways. Often the arrival time is the same by either route, but even when the freeway is decidedly faster, traveling the side roads makes for a more adventuresome journey. We still arrive at the same destination, the end of our journey. The difference lies in the quality of our lives. Traveling on the less populated roads, moving indirectly toward our goals, not only opens options but allows for an individually tailored life experience.

Tactic—Find an Understaffed Company

An understaffed organization is one in which there aren't enough people to do everything that needs doing. This means opportunity—opportunity to gain essential hands-on experience, often without having to change your job classification. Opportunities to experiment and showcase your accomplishments abound. Let's take a closer look.

Less Competition

Consider a simple example. Bill wants to play on a high school football team. While quick to learn, and well coordinated, Bill is an average player. Although he wouldn't be considered physically big by most standards — 5'11" and 175 pounds, he's one of the bigger guys in his senior class of 100 students.

Suppose John, Bill's identical twin attends a different school, where there are 1000 kids in his class instead of only 100. John, too, aspires to be on the football team. Both Bill and John are somewhat shy and feel self-conscious as they try out for their respective teams. One makes it, the other doesn't. Who makes the team?

Easier to Meet Standards

Bill makes the team. Why? The selection pool is much less in the small school. Bill's coach doesn't have a lot of boys from whom to choose, so the acceptance criteria are easier to meet. To the coach in a small school, Bill looks like a good candidate. He's big, he's smart, and he's motivated. In fact, there's a good chance that if Bill hadn't tried out, the coach would have tried to persuade him to do so.

In contrast, John hardly gets a moment's consideration from the big school coach. There's nothing outstanding about John, and there are many bigger, more qualified boys to pick from, all eager to play. The big school coach can be picky. He can raise his acceptance criteria. John is rejected and his football career ends before ever starting.

Opportunity to Develop

For Bill, on the other hand, it's just the beginning. Being accepted for the team builds Bill's confidence. He throws himself into practice, and he learns fast. Since Bill's coach can't afford to lose him, he gives Bill a lot of encouragement. Bill's skills and confidence grow under the glow of the coach's attention.

Success breeds success. Bill excels. Girls think he's a hunk, while his twin, John, watches with pride and envy. Bill refines his skills, he stands out. He is the area all-star. At graduation, Bill looks forward to college football and an athletic scholarship, something he never dreamed possible that day he tried out, so long ago.

Because Bill's small school was an understaffed organization, Bill had an opportunity to play football on the team. In the process, he had a chance to develop his skills, to build confidence, to learn to take risks—and to develop a track record.

By comparison, John's school was overstaffed. As a result he experienced failure at try out, did not make the team, so he didn't have the opportunity Bill had to develop confidence or gain experience. Bill graduated with an I-Can-Do identity; John graduated with a Nothing-Special identity. Bill is likely to take risks in the future because he's learned he can rise to the challenge and is confident that he will succeed.

Loose Boundaries

Understaffed organizations are more fluid than are organizations in which every job and task is filled. Also distinctions between jobs are blurred in understaffed organizations. Often a situation will arise in which there is a deadline and, as is usually the case, there is not enough staff to do everything. This is an opportunity. If you have *some* skill in performing the needed task, you are quickly recruited. You are an eager, able body. Able bodies are needed and eagerness counts.

In an understaffed organization, you'll have a chance to learn and refine your skills. If you lack sufficient experience or the required education, look for the understaffed organization. It can be your big break!

Change Your Labels

Because the linear strategy of climbing the corporate ladder is so all pervasively accepted, we often get trapped on a track, unable to get off. We are labeled with a job classification. And once we have that label, it sticks to us, restricting our movement.

One of the hardest labels to shake for example, is secretary. In fact, the ambiguous administrative assistant title has practically replaced it. As soon as the personnel officer, employment counselor, or prospective boss sees "secretary" on a resume, the applicant is categorized and slotted, not considered for anything but a secretarial position. If you want to switch tracks, to change your job label, position yourself in an understaffed organization.

Tracy's Story

When I went to work as a receptionist for a toy manufacturer, I had a lot of ambition and drive but little training or experience. Receptionist was nowhere, but it was a toehold—a start. I decided I'd be the best receptionist I could, and it paid off. In the course of answering the phones, and taking messages, I developed a "phone relationship" with most of the accounts.

After a few months they needed someone to process orders. I was a natural choice since I knew the accounts. And in less than a year, I was promoted again, this time to assistant sales manager because I was the only one who knew all the accounts and who ordered what. After several months I got antsy so I sent out my resume and snared a position as sales manager in TufChairs, a leading office furniture manufacturer. I've come a long way from receptionist!

Dan's Story

I'd been knocking around in publishing for a couple of years when I joined a small press as a freelance editor. In a matter of months I was on the payroll as a full-time editor. At the time, there was no in-house promotion. I knew next to nothing about it. But then no one else did either. So I began doing PR for our books.

> *Well, I got good at it, and I discovered I liked promotion. And I developed a good reputation for myself. Two and a half years later, I took the position of marketing director for a large prestigious specialty-publishing house. Now that's on the job training!*

More Accepting

Understaffed organizations have another positive feature: People in such organizations are typically more accepting of differences, while people in overstaffed organizations are often cliquish, with in-groups and outgroups. If you want to feel like you belong, that you're an essential member of the team, look for an understaffed organization.

But there is a dark side as well. Understaffed organizations tend to be stressful environments in a constant state of change and chaos. You must be comfortable with chaos to excel in an understaffed organization.

Tactic—Take a Vaguely Defined Position

The position that allows the maximum leeway is the one that is vaguely defined. Clearly defined jobs have parameters, guidelines, and standards and the way-we-do-it rules. Accountability is built in. A clear definition of what is expected of you makes it easy to measure your performance. You know what you are to do and so does your employer.

Clarity of job description provides an objective basis for evaluation and acknowledgement. Clearly defining jobs is considered good management, but when the definition focuses on how functions are to be performed instead of what is to be achieved, definitions can become constrictions.

Before accepting any position or assignment, ronin look over job descriptions. They favor those that specify *what* us to be produced and avoid those that spell out *how*. Because ronin are capable self-managers, comfortable with ambiguity, and able to create structure, they seek out vaguely defined jobs in key positions.

The absence of limits, definitions, and standards of evaluation, is a window of opportunity allowing you to create the definitions, set the limits, to determine the standards of evaluation—and to expand your territory.

The vaguely defined job has its perils. But its virtue is that you can make it what you want. You can define it and redefine it. But you must be able to create structure in a vacuum to do so.

Chapter 15

STRATEGY
Concentrated
Dispersion

You rise in a feudal organization by leaving your present job and taking another at the next level within the company or by changing companies. In either case, upward progress is made one step upward at a time.

You can bypass the ladder by using an expansion tactic, in which responsibilities are expanded by gradually enveloping people and functions. The strategy is to retain control of old responsibilities while simultaneously adding on responsibilities and titles.

Tactic—Expand, Don't Climb

Instead of climbing rungs, look for boring or difficult projects to take over, those no one else wants. These are *unattached problems*—problems that belong to no one and are free for the taking. When you take them as yours, your territory grows. Soon you have more freedom and you don't have to ask permission.

> To ask
> is to seek denial.
>
> —*Scott McNealy*
> FOUNDER & CEO
> SUN MICROSYSTEMS

Expand into areas that involve liaison and communication between departments. Look for territories that are central to the operations of the corporation, such as sales in a manufacturing company or loans in a bank. Power follows money, so stay close to the flow of money. For example, becoming a line manager of a profit center opens up more territory than becoming a higher paid staff administrator.

Analyze your formal job description. Can you make a legitimate claim to the function you are eyeing? If so, you might be able to assume it de facto. If the function is currently performed by someone else, review your job description with your boss and ask that the function be transferred to be under your direction. Don't move precipitously, however. First, assess your competitive strength and prepare your case.

Establish a Presence

When the expansion area lies out side your job description, begin by establishing a presence. Place a stone in the area by working as a collaborator on a project within someone else's responsibility. Another approach is to assign members of your staff to projects under other's jurisdiction so that they serve as extensions of your influence within the corporation. Using this expansion tactic, you can identify gaps in no man's land. Then assign your people to work on the unassigned, vaguely defined functions.

The promotion ladder only exists as long as people believe in it, and are willing to trudge up it.... Each step taken...[in your rise in the hierarchy]...means abandoning the one below it, just as you have to take your foot off rung A of a ladder to place it on rung B. This kind of promotion requires a great deal of time, and the competition for each rung is severe. Worse, you have to abandon what you have in order to reach for what you want, thus increasing your chance of falling off and landing back on the heap, at the foot of the ladder. And you are planning your career in terms of an existing and rigid structure, which means you're playing according to someone else's rules.

—Michael Korda
POWER!
HOW TO GET IT, HOW TO KEEP IT

Link Functions Up

Periodically, link up the functions you have acquired into a coherent project tied into your job description, which you rewrite to accommodate the expansion. Connect disconnected functions into a territory, to strengthen your authority over it. At an appropriate time, consolidate your acquisition by asking for an official appointment of title for the acquired duties.

Defend Inroads

If someone makes a strong inroad into your sphere of influence, it is best not to confront the spearhead directly. Instead, like a martial arts master, like a ronin, use the momentum of the invader's thrust to throw him off balance.

Fall back to a solid position that is well integrated into your main function and tied to a core interest of the company. Draw the invader into your sphere of influence. When the invader is extended well beyond his or her designated functions, take your case to the common boss, requesting a formal transfer of tasks, projects, personnel, and resources to your jurisdiction. And make sure your job description is updated to clarify your authority over the disputed territory.

Tactic—Generalize with Specialties

Our world is changing; things are no longer predictable. Futurists say we are at one of those points we read about in history books—the transition from one era to another. Computers, acting both as catalyst and as a means, are catapulting us into an Information Society that promises to be vastly different from the Industrial Society of our youth.

This is no time to put all your stones in one corner, as Black did. At best, specialization wins a small niche that once meant professional and economic security, but no longer. Now specialization leads to disintermediation and obsolescence. In uncertain times, diversify. That's the rule of thumb.

The ability to adapt and change is the key to survival, success, and fulfillment. Limited in range of knowledge and skill, the specialist is inflexible—hence vulnerable. What, for example, does a professor of Latin and Sanskrit do when college enrollment drops and along with it the demand for professors of classical languages?

Even if your current position is mainstream, you cannot expect to remain in the same job or profession for life. Instead of specializing, prepare for an uncertain future by becoming a generalist with specialties.

Broad Focus

Versatility—having many skills and many areas of knowledge—is a prerequisite of adaptability because it provides the maximum advantage when confronted with the uncertainty of change. For example, the Japanese *ronin* did not stare fixedly at one, small spot on his opponent, but instead used a soft, diffuse focus, taking in all of his opponent so he was ready to counter a blow from any direction.

Generalizable Skills

Modern day ronin have many hats and are masters of generalizable skills that apply across specialties to a wide range of endeavors. The most generalizable skills are people skills—communicating, negotiating, interviewing, organizing, motivating teaching, and directing; problem solving skills—observing, researching, analyzing, and evaluation; thinking skills—inductive and deductive logic and categorizing; as well as many others. These are like the many ways to cut that the Japanese *ronin* practiced and perfected. *Ronin* were professional warriors who specialized in more than one weapon. For any particular battle, they could choose to use the long sword or the short sword or both.

But *ronin's* expertise was not limited to fighting. Trained as samurai, they were skilled in brush painting, and composing poetry, educated in the philosophy of their time, and disciplined in meditation. While *doing ronin*, some became writers, Confucian scholars, or schoolteachers; some taught swordsmanship or other military arts; others traded on their ability with their weapons and hired themselves out as bodyguards and troubleshooters for rich merchants.

Similarly, modern ronin are multi-skilled, having a variety of hats to wear. They often operate within a broad professional field, such as law, psychology, business, or publishing, but resist narrowing into one specialty. Being secure in their ability to adapt, ronin welcome change as an opportunity to learn and create. For ronin, having flexibility means security. Times of doing ronin are accepted as opportunities to tackle more challenges and acquire greater skills.

> *The vacational vocation is the vocational vacation.*
>
> —*So and So*

Increase Degrees of Freedom

Whenever contemplating any move, always consider the strategic degrees of freedom such a move will provide. That is, how many opportunities or paths to your goal are opened up by the move?

Tactic—Intersect Specialties

As the game of Go progresses, if the players continue their original strategies, Black will strengthen the hold on his corner, while White's influence expands and arenas that once seemed divergent, begin to converge. By the end of the game, White will dominate most of the board and win.

By employing the dual strategies of *indirection* and *concentrated dispersion* in our career planning, we can often merge two or more specialties. The point where our specialties, including avocational interests, intersect is an area of strength and advantage. Not only do we have a broad foundation and the mystique of being different, we also have the advantage of a broader perspective and reduced competition. Chances are there are few, if any, other people with your unique mix of skills, knowledge and wisdom.

In the monologue Max describes using this strategy with his career in law and engineering. Although there are thousands of engineers and thousands of legal researchers, relatively few are knowledgeable and skilled in both. By intersecting his specialties Max elevated himself from the status of average and put himself at the head of the competition.

Max's Story

After 10 years in engineering, I was burned out. I couldn't relate to my colleagues because they had such a limited view of everything. I felt socially cut off. So after my divorce, I quit my job and dropped out. At first I withdrew and did nothing for a while. A friend who volunteered for a Neighborhood Legal Assistance Center convinced me to volunteer, too. It was fascinating and I enjoyed it. I discovered I could use a number of my engineering skills in the legal research: logical thinking, how to use the library, how to solve problems, how to make an argument. Before long, I was the number one volunteer legal researcher. Eventually there was an opening for a paid position and I got it even though I had no formal training in law at all. I worked for The Center for about three years, and although I couldn't go to court, I did do legal counseling. I liked the involvement with people.

Eventually I had made enough contacts and had developed enough skill and confidence that I was easily able to become a freelance legal research consultant, so I left The Center. During the next two years, I built up a substantial clientele. I did O.K. But it was a feast or famine situation. So when a large prestigious law firm in the City approached me with an offer, I jumped at it. They needed someone with expertise in both engineering and law. Well, I got the job. Now I have what I like about engineering and what I like about law and I make a lot more money, too. The smartest thing I ever did was listening to my inner voice and leave engineering.

Tactic—Composite Career

Doing the same general activity 40 hours a week for years numbs imagination and ambition, thwarting development. You can break out of this rut with a composite career, in which you perform different functions for different employers. A composite career is, in essence, an array of part-time positions. This strategy offers variety and a breath of fresh air to those whose full-time classification is restricted to one function.

Vocational Pathfinding

A composite career is often made up of modules of one function, such as accounting and bookkeeping, performed in one work environment, and another function, such as selling software packages, performed in a different work environment. E-lancers and free agents have a sort of composite career. Of composite careerists, William Bridges, author of *Transitions*, says, "They actually represent a social phenomenon of great importance. They are vocational pathfinders of a new workforce."

A composite career can serve as a buffer, making you less vulnerable to the whims of the economy. In economic hard times, you will have a broad strong foundation—your stones are not all in one corner. Just as capital investment managers and corporations diversify their portfolios, you too can increase security by diversifying job involvements. Even if one or more pieces of your composite are lost, you still have others for support.

An equally important benefit is the enhanced feelings of personal power and control over your work life. Work in one setting provides relief from the others, so rather than getting tired of the work, you return refueled. Should one of the jobs turn sour and threaten to become a burnout situation, you can leave with relative ease because you are not faced with an all or nothing situation and forced to choose between putting up with the intolerable or standing in the unemployment line.

Ease of Transition

Composite careers can also serve as a transition and exploration step, a way of ferreting out the intersection of your specialties. Starting off with a part-time commitment in one specialty, another in a second specialty, perhaps yet another in a third area of interest, you may be able to bring the divergent activities together into a hybrid of your specialties in which you offer a unique and sought after serve or product.

Using this modular strategy of being on the payroll of more than one company can be the beginning of a transition into becoming an entrepreneur or consultant—never again an employee. Composite careers

Even if you don't operate a business, you're in a better position if you act as a supplier of a service rather then as an employee. You can contract with companies to perform specific services for them at specific prices. In addition to the tax benefits, you can choose your own working hours, usually make more money, and have more free time.

—*Harry Browne*
How I Found Freedom in an Unfree World

offer freedom, flexibility in activities and scheduling as well as an opportunity for balance.

Ramona's Story

There are four things that are of vital interest to me: dancing, religion, children and being a mother. And I've managed to work them all into my career in a very satisfying way by having more than one job. I earn most of my money three nights a week as a professional showgirl dancing in one of the big clubs. It's a lot of fin. I love the glamour, the glitter, and the audience. And they love me.

My second job is the one that surprises most. Every Sunday I teach a Bible class for preschoolers. Some think it's odd, my being a showgirl and all. But there is nothing immoral about being a dancer. I have had no problems with the parents, either. In fact, a lot of them have come to see me dance. And the kids love me.

In the afternoon twice a week, I teach dance to sixth graders in one of the local schools. That leaves most of my days free, allowing me to be a good mother. As I said, I'm very happy with my combination of jobs. It allows me to satisfy all my needs. I don't' have to sacrifice anything.

Chapter 16

STRATEGY
Maintain the Initiative

 In the game of Go, *sente* refers to certain carefully placed offensive moves by one player that demand a defensive response from the opponent. For examples, suppose Black is heavily invested in one corner but has not yet secured it, and White places a stone two squares away, threatening to jump in underneath Black. This maneuver forces Black to use his next turn to defend against White's offensive moves. White maintains the initiative because on her next turn she has more options. She can continue the penetration into Black's territory or she can place a stone elsewhere instead.

Act, Don't React

Rather than wait to be told what to do, ronin take the initiative. For example, Sophie, an editor, noticed the growing interest in electronic publishing. She also noted many larger bookstores were starting to carry lines of e-books. The indicators suggested that electronic publishing is the wave of the future. Rather than waiting until her boss told her to investigate the feasibility of expanding into e-publishing and distribution, she took the initiative.

Sophie educated herself by going to computer conventions, reading computer trade magazines, and talking to distributors and bookstores as well as to other publishers. She then put together and presented the Board of Directors with a strong proposal, arguing the benefits of converting the backlist into e-books. After much debate and consideration, a new department was formed—headed by Sophie.

> *Those who desire personal power are very different. Instead of controlling a portion of the existing world, they set out to create their own.*
>
> —*Michael Korda*
> *Power!*
> *How to Get It, How to Use It*

You can maintain the initiative in your career and on the job by positioning yourself so that you act, rather than react. Endeavor to be the cause of events, not at the mercy of them.

Self-Start

Heroism, according to the Danish philosopher Kirkegarrd, lies in the act of making a beginning. Starting is difficult; it takes courage. At the beginning of an endeavor, especially when it is outside the conventional mold, we don't know if it will be well received or if we will succeed. We may fall short and be ridiculed.

Another force that impedes starting is inertia. Physics law of inertia says that a body at rest tends to stay at rest. Before starting, we are a body at rest and must overcome inertia to get going.

Small Steps

Starting is always easier when you proceed in incremental steps. A step can be as small as writing a list and you have started and made a beginning. Steps should be small enough that you can achieve them with little effort. Once started, continue taking small steps to keep the momentum going.

Keep Starting

Inevitably, we wind down and stop. Expect this. It is easy to get sidetracked. You may have to set the project aside to attend to other matters. Sometimes motivation wanes and you just peter out. Always have a plan for making another beginning. Remember to use small steps. Do some small action to push the project forward. You may even have to have a plan to make a beginning each day—sometimes more than once a day. Bringing a project to completion is less about thinking about the end point than it is about beginning again and again.

Do More

To be in a strong position to carve out a new project or to take over a territory you must simultaneously complete everything that is already within your area of responsibility. This means that you must do more than the person in the next desk does and have a do-what-it-takes attitude rather than I-just-do-my-job-description attitude.

Determine Your Direction

When you have broken the inertia and are moving the next challenge is determining where are you going. Without a direction you are likely to go around and around, working constantly—being busy—but accomplishing little and getting nowhere.

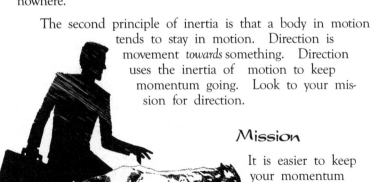

The second principle of inertia is that a body in motion tends to stay in motion. Direction is movement *towards* something. Direction uses the inertia of motion to keep momentum going. Look to your mission for direction.

Mission

It is easier to keep your momentum going when you know your purpose and see yourself achieving it, than when plodding along, putting one foot ahead of the other one wondering where you are going. A mission is an overriding purpose. It is the predominant objective to be accomplished. A mission is like a goal but a lot more.

We tend to think of a job as a series of tasks that someone else has assigned us to do. This view of work makes us myopic, focused on the details without seeing the big picture. In the process we lose sight of the purpose of our efforts.

Every job has a purpose. All jobs are created to cope with a problem. Activities that reliably solve a problem are systemized into a "job." When you know the problem you were hired to solve you know your mission in your organization. Solving the problem you were hired to solve is your purpose and the reason to carry out your job functions.

> *Every problem you can solve means more money for you. A problem is a market for a solution. Be sensitive to the problems of everyone you do business with.*
>
> —*Harry Browne,*
> How I Found Freedom in an Unfree World

Identify the Problem You Were Hired to Solve

You can identify the problem that your job solves by examining what would happen if no one did your job and it was left completely neglected. Do this in your imagination. Imagine that no one is dealing with the problem that is yours to solve. Imagine that your job is left undone. Carry the scenario to the extreme and watch what happens. This exercise reveals your problem—your territory on the game board.

For example, take the problem that receptionists have traditionally solved. Suppose no one is handling that problem and that there is no voice mail. Imagine what would happen. The phone rings endlessly unanswered until callers give up in frustration. Customers call to place orders but no one answers or the person who answers is not an order taker, so they take their business elsewhere.

People are confused and annoyed—you get the picture. Imagining this scenario just briefly shows how important it is that the problem of answering, screening and routing calls be well solved. Interestingly, receptionist is one of those functions that is being disintermediated, with the problem being solved by white-collar robots that we now call voice mail.

Stop for a moment and consider your central job function. Imagine that it is being neglected and that no one is handling it. Take the scenario to the extreme and you will see a picture of the problem that is yours to solve. Solving this problem is your mission—within the organization where you work. Knowing your mission is valuable because it tells you why you were hired and what you are to accomplish.

Work Smarter

Most of us have heard the edict "work smarter, not harder." The person who works harder works longer and longer, taking work home and going to the office on weekends. Working longer and doing more is not a feasible way to deal with having too much work and not enough time to do it.

Instead we must work smarter. Obviously if you have too much to do and not enough time to do it, some things are going to be left undone. Further, the world is changing and work is changing, Adapting to change requires that we start doing new things and that we stop doing certain old things. The dilemma is knowing what to do and what to leave undone.

Audit Your Functions

Compile a list of your activities by conducting an audit. Here's how: every fifteen minutes, on the quarter of the hour, jot down what you are doing. Continue doing this for several days to identify your activities and what percentage of your time you devote to each.

Apply Leverage

A lever is a tool that enables us is to use less effort to achieve a greater gain—which is working smarter. You can apply leverage to your job to work smarter. One by one, rate how much impact each activity that you identified in the audit has upon you achieving your mission—the problem you were hired to solve. Rate the impact from 1 to 5, with 1 being "little or no impact" and with 5 being "great impact." Evaluate each activity identified in the audit in this way.

Activities you rated as 1 and 2 are candidates for being left undone. Activities that you rated 4 and 5 are high leverage activities. These are the activities that have the greatest impact upon achieving your mission and solving the problem you were hired to solve. By concentrating on high leverage activities you work smarter even though there are activities that you leave undone.

Vision

The way that you find your vision is by seeing your mission achieved, by seeing the problem you were hired to solve solved. Don't worry about the steps in between or how you will get to the solution that you envision. Brainstorm all the ways that that problem could be solved, that your mission might be achieved. Picture the problem solved. This picture is your "vision"—the image of your mission accomplished. When you see a solution that you can achieve from where you are in your job and that fits with your values, use this as your vision—the picture of the end point towards which you will aim. It is the beacon you sail towards or the North Star you use to navigate.

Mental Practice

It helps to exercise your mental skills in finding possibilities and opportunities that you might do. Make it a practice to think of things that you might take into your job function. Imagine steps to achieve your mission and ways to alter your work. Mull over alternative career paths. Make liberal use of your imagination.

Imagine Businesses and Projects

As an exercise, when hearing of a new trend imagine a business that you could create to capitalize upon it. The objective is to exercise your imagination in an applied way. At some time you may have looked at magazines about redecorating homes and then imagined how you might use the principles that you read about to redecorate your living room. It is a similar kind of mental exercise that keeps your creativity sharp.

Look for Unattached Problems

Unattached problems are problem that are being neglected and belong in no one's territory. Often they are the dreary tasks that are pushed aside and pile up. Sometimes they are a by-product of disintermediation. For example, as voice mail replaces receptionists, callers not being personally greeted may be a free-floating problem—or opportunity. When you take over an unattached problem that is something that you can solve, you expand your territory. As your territory grows, you can make a legitimate case for needing additional personnel to manage it.

Find a Need and Fill It

Looking for needs and imagining ways that those needs can be met is another way of exercising your applied creativity. It develops a keen eye and exercises your strategic thinking. When you find a need that is an adjunct to your job function, you can take it over and expand your territory.

Create Structure

Work flows best in structure. When you self-start and create a new project, eventually it must be structured if it is to be passed on to someone else as a defined function to carry out. Organizations are masterful at structuring work, with their hierarchies and more recently with the introductions of teams. Structure involves breaking projects into pieces and creating job functions and then sequencing the steps, for example. Delegating is important so that you do not do everything yourself. Instead you structure it, then pass it on for others to maintain.

Chapter 17

STRATEGY
Concentrate on Key Factors

 Following a track in the same way as others who are competing for positions in your field yields no competitive edge. Instead, identify those areas that are decisive for success in your particular line of work, add the right combination of skills and experience, you may be able to put yourself in a position of real competitive superiority. But first, you must identify the key factors for success. Then devise a plan to invest your resources and efforts in a way most likely to develop superior strength in the key areas.

Tactic—Conduct a Product Analysis

Categorizing the market is preliminary to deciding where to concentrate your efforts. The easiest way to do this is to make a product market matrix. List your products down the side of a sheet of blank paper. Your products are what you offer—skills you have, results you can deliver, or services you can provide. Next, divide the market into categories and list them across the top of the paper. Your market categories might be different users of your service, or organizational needs, as examples.

For example, Cheryl Lynn had been running the flea market for a local community college for several years. Her mother, in the course of fund raising for the Junior League, had coordinated many events. The pair got along well and decided to give a joint venture a try. They wanted to put on some kind of faire but were not sure what. So they started by making a product market matrix. On the vertical axis Cheryl Lynn listed possible themes for events that they could produce; on the horizontal axis she listed their target markets.

An interactive online development trade show for career women interested them the most and seemed to have the greatest potential for making money. Alternatively, they thought a technical trade show focused on the needs of the handicapped might be a winner because they lived in an area with a high population of independently living handicapped people. Having identified these two potential ventures, Cheryl Lynn and her mother began researching the needs of each market.

Markets

	Professionals	Laypeople	Special Interest
Sale of used items	Office equipment recycle sale	Flea market	Photography swap meet
Computer trade show	Software trade show for business women	Computer games trade show	Display of technological aids for handicapped
Craft or cultural show	Office art display	Street crafts fair	Art show by handicapped artists

Products: Skills and Services

PRODUCT–MARKET MATRIX

Tactic— Compare Winners & Losers

Another method for identifying where to concentrate your efforts is to compare people who have achieved a goal similar to yours and those who have tried but failed. The object is to identify the differences and similarities between the groups in order to determine what winners did that helped them win that losers did not do. And the reverse is important as well. Look for what losers did that contributed to their failure that winners avoided doing.

Greg, for example, was a systems analyst for a small mid-western city and

The Arrivers and Derailers Compared

In the first place, derailed executives had a series of successes, but usually in similar kinds of situations. They had turned two businesses around, or managed progressively larger jobs in the same function. By contrast, the arrivers had more diversity in their successes; they had turned a business around and successfully moved from line to staff and back, or started a new business from scratch and completed a special assignment with distinction. They built plants in the wilderness and the Amazonian Jungle, salvaged disastrous operations, resolved all out wars between corporate divisions without bloodshed. One even built a town.

—Morgan W. M. McCall, Jr.
—Michael M. Lombardo
"WHAT MAKES A TOP EXECUTIVE"
PSYCHOLOGY TODAY

wanted to move to the fast paced Silicon Valley. So did a lot of others. The competition was stiff. He called companies where he had sent resumes and asked about the qualifications of people who were actually hired and he learned that those most often brought in from out of state had systems analysis experience. Based on that knowledge, Greg made a lateral transfer to a local company that needed a system analyst. Two years later, he landed a position in a fast growing Silicon Valley company.

Chapter 18

STRATEGY
Ride Trends;
Avoid Fads

Predicting the course of events— forecasting trends—is as important in determining where to place our career stones as it is in deciding which of thousands of issues in the stock market to purchase. Obviously, we want to move into areas with the most opportunity and growth potential.

Accepting a job position or undertaking training in a specialty that turns out to be a fad can result in serious losses and setbacks. At one point, for example, the price of silver shot up almost 500 percent in a matter of a few months. But to the despair of most investors, it was a fad that ended abruptly when the price dropped to the pre-fad level within a couple of days. By contrast, those who invested in selected software issues profited by riding a trend. By the end of the Century software had become the fastest growing industry in the world.

Ability to distinguish between a fad and a trend is essential in planning career moves. But what do we look for? First off, fads are short term. Like a comet, they dazzle for a few months. True, money can be made and quick advancement achieved by riding fads, but it's risky and the stakes are high. To capitalize on a fad, you must call it right as well as be in the right place at the right time. While fads take off fast, only those in on the first wave usually profit. Fads are almost always get rich schemes where most jump on too late and get fleeced instead.

Trends on the other hand, build momentum slowly. Timing is important but not critical. Actually being in on the beginning of a trend is not usually the best position. Trends allow time to analyze, consider, and plan optimal moves. As the trend expands and speeds up, opportunities multiply. Even if you delay until after the peak, you are still likely to profit from your invested efforts. Another difference is that trends plateau, whereas fads dive. Electronic publishing is a trend that began in the 1980s and grew steadily until it accelerated exponentially in the first decade of the century.

Typically, fads originate from one source. Trends, on the other hand, come from many sources, beginning in many places at the same time, like grass roots. There is no one to root, no one master-mind, no one catalyst behind the software industry or e-books, for example.

> *Trends, like horses, are easier to ride in the direction they are already going.*
> —John Nesbitt
> MEGATRENDS

Email is an example of a megatrend that exploded into our lives in the last years of the Century. It began many years earlier among high level scientists who used it to communicate. Slowly and steadily it grew. There are no latecomers because email is here to stay.

Tactic—Look for Intersections

The point at which two industries or two vital functions converge is the intersection. That convergence often creates friction that spells opportunity—a problem that needs fixing. If you can devise a way to mesh gears of divergent concerns smoothly—to provide a clutch so to speak—you have a shot at dominating a whole new territory. You'll gain a lot of freedom and probably a lot of money as well.

At the intersection, there are opportunities for both entrepreneurs and "intrapreneurs," who function entrepreneurially inside the corporation as well as for e-lancers to develop new services or pro,ducts, to add new territory to the game board, and to increase autonomy.

Plentiful Opportunities

There are infinite possible intersections. Some are more fertile and have more potential than others. The conjunction of two, or more, initially divergent components of a trend which is where an intersection that has long term potential is found. If the trend is a strong one, there is potential for the intersection to expand into a full-fledged industry.

Tactic—Find the Rift

What's a rift? It's a big tear in the fabric of the rules that we live by. It's a mental change in the game, one that creates a bunch of new losers— and a handful of new winners.

—Seth Godin

Personal computers for professionals, for example, have been simultaneously a godsend—and a nightmare. The machine is great; the software a marvel. But learning to get online, load software, set up websites, catch viruses and keep up can be an ordeal for non-techies. The manuals are overwhelming and still substantially incomprehensible. Software writers speak computereze, not English. What the hell is a scuzzy port? A gif? A cookie? Fortunes have been made in that intersection. Ronin, the wave men, have been quick to move in with user-friendly software manuals and using names like TechKnight, make home calls to reinstall crashed systems, all while holding hysterical hands.

Another thriving intersection is the mailing list industry, between mail order retailers and buyers. With the explosion of e-marketing and promotional websites mail list sellers could be another business going the way of the buggy whip. Those selling quality emailing lists to businesses are in the position to move into a new intersection—between small businesses and e-lancers. In fact, as we move into the Information Era, sales of information will become an increasingly profitable venture. So look for an intersection—it means opportunity.

Chapter 19

STRATEGY
Get Visibility

 It doesn't take too many months in the workplace to realize that good work alone brings a few promotions or merit raises, but it is not likely to win much influence or gain significant territory in the World Game. Being well positioned and seen is essential to expand your sphere of influence. The modest strategy of waiting to be noticed, more often than not, leads to invisibility.

Visibility does not come by chance, but as a direct result of how people present themselves. Some are shy, while others find the notion of self–presentation distasteful because it feels like selling oneself. But self–presentation need not be forced or fake. The fact is we are presenting ourselves all the time anyway. No matter what we do or how we act, it's a presentation upon which others make judgments that can aid or hinder our career progress.

Tactic—Articulate Your Skills

Amazing as it may seem, many people cannot describe their skills—clearly and concisely. When asked, they describe ways they've used their skills, leaving the skills themselves implied which leaves the listener with the task of distilling the skills from the list of functions performed.

The danger is that the listener may not be clever enough or interested enough to identify your skills. Why give up your power in this way? Articulate your skills and do so within the listener's frame of reference. That is, translate your skills into the listener's language, one that speaks to the listener's needs.

Tactic—Demonstrate Your Skills

Seeing is believing, and one of the most effective ways to present your best self is to show, rather than tell. Seek out situations in which you can show others what you can do. Watch for opportunities to arrange the conditions so that the people you want to impress "catch" you performing rather than you telling them how great you are.

At work, remember that you are not merely carrying out a function, and not merely earning money, you are also demonstrating, moment by moment, what you can do. Embrace every task. No matter how routine it is or how mundane it may seem—as an opportunity to demonstrate your excellence!

Tactic—Serve Associations

Think of association meetings you've attended. Who stands out? Which people do you remember? Chances are it's the officers—the people who stand up at every meeting. By serving associations as a committee member or officer you create an opportunity to demonstrate what you can do and to learn and refine new skills. In short, by serving associations you can create your own learning lab in which to teach yourself how to lead while putting yourself in a position of visibility.

Tactic—showcase accomplishments

Modesty is admirable in many situations, but some people take it to an extreme and literally hide their accomplishments. Don't do that! That's like passing your turn in the game and putting no stones on the board at all. Those who are overly modest subscribe to the erroneous belief that worthy accomplishments automatically bring deserved recognition.

> To be a great leader is to be a shaman. You must be seasoned in the art of using images to instill an unshaken belief among your followers that you will always succeed in whatever you undertake.
>
> —R.G.H. Siu
> THE CRAFT OF POWER

Ralph's Story

A big investment outfit wanted to put in a shopping enter near here. Well, a bunch of us got upset and formed an ad hoc committee to study the environmental impact. We were going to take it to the County. It took months and I ended up doing most of it—the interviews, collecting articles, doing research in the library, and gathering stats. I put most of the report together, too. I wrote about 80 percent of the articles and did all of the layout and typing. You could say I was the force behind it all. But everyone who worked on it got credit, even if his or her contribution was small, I saw to that! I listed everyone's name in alphabetical order—including mine, too. Well, we succeeded in blocking the shopping center and I'm really proud of that report. The experience turned my head around. I think I would like to get into local politics though I don't know how to start.

Ralph hid his accomplishment when he could have just as easily used it to jump-start a political career. By being overly modest, you put roadblocks in your own path, close off your opportunities and sabotage your motivation.

Don't wait to be noticed and acknowledged. Don't give your power to others. People are too busy and too absorbed in their own situations. Find a way to showcase your accomplishments. Ask that your name be on products and associated with services you provide. You may not get credit everytime, but you can be sure you'll rarely get credit without asking for it. Speak up and tell others about your accomplishments. Send a news release to the public relations people at corporate headquarters. They may run it in the company paper or even place a story in a local paper. Why? Because your accomplishments makes them look good.

The same is true of associations that you belong to as well as all the groups you're involved with. Everyone loves a winner. Inform the secretary of your local association about your accomplishment. Perhaps he or she will place a notice about it in the association newsletter. Be creative. Seek out ways to bring your accomplishments to center stage. Showcasing your accomplishments makes your company look good and advances you in the World Game.

Tactic—Publish

Publishing is a powerful way to present yourself and your accomplishments. Your name, as author in print, and the aura of "expert" that it brings, increases confidence as your credibility grows in the eyes of colleagues. Think of each article you publish as a stone placed on the World Game board. With each stone you place you enlarge your sphere of influence.

By writing the book, *Overcoming Job Burnout*, for example, I became an identified "expert" on how to overcome worker malaise, thereby increasing my sphere of influence and capturing new territory. Spheres of influence can be based on status, authority, knowledge, and wealth.

One of the easiest ways to start is online. As they say, "content is king." If you have a web site, post your articles and make sure to register each one with major search engines. Then put an automatic footnote in your email with a link to your site or new article. Soon web publishers will find your articles and put links to them, or even ask to post them on their sites. If you don't have your own site, you can offer your material to sites that feature related information. You'll be surprised at how many takers you get.

Tactic—Teach

Opportunities to teach abound. Continuing education for adults, another trend growing rapidly online, is the frontier of education. Virtually every community college and university has an extended education program offering practical one day and evening courses. You can create a workshop around just about any skill you have.

Assess Your Teachable Skills

Make a list of possible skills and subjects in which you have expertise. Don't restrict yourself to academic topics. Think of life skills like mothering, gardening, and doing handyman repairs, for example. Check offerings in your local college catalog and brainstorm ways to package your skills into a teachable topic that's not listed. Prepare a course proposal and send it to the program director. It's easier than you imagine, and the benefits you'll reap can be many.

In addition to the satisfaction of teaching and what you learn while doing it, you'll make vital contacts from a position of expert. Teaching brings visibility. Your course, name, and bio will be printed in the college catalog, which is sent to thousands of people, as well as to hundreds of personnel departments.

Colleges are only one the only market for courses.
There are high school adult education programs,
community centers, associations and online universities. Additionally, courses are offered outside of formal
schools, by organizations like The Learning Annex, for
example, which offers short courses in hotels on a
variety of practical topics. Freelance community
schools like The Open Exchange and Common
Ground, where for a small fee, you can list your class
and teach it in your living room or back yard.

If your course is free, practical, and focused on a
vital topic, you'll get a lot of takers. Eventually, you
can charge, sometimes quite handsomely. Teaching can
pull in consulting gigs, too, which can provide a nice
financial buffer, add variety to your work, as well as
make a nonlinear career move possible. Teaching
provides an opportunity to place a stone in new territory.

Tactic—Give Speeches

Look at your game board. What territory of expertise have you captured? What do you know about?
What can you do? Chances are there are a lot of people
who need the information and skills you have. Speaking can be a lot of fun. As you get better you'll go to
interesting retreats in places like Martha's Vineyards or
Las Vegas while being well paid, too.

Whether a beginner or seasoned speaker, you'll
probably want to join the National Speakers Association that has chapters in most states. Check the 800-
phone directory for listings in your area. The format of
their meetings provides an opportunity to build re-
warding relationships, learn valuable speaking tips,
observe speakers at all skill levels, as well as to have
the opportunity to speak before a group yourself.

Everyone Has Something to Teach

Job: Mechanic
Possible Presentation: Ten-point checklist of evaluating a used car before you buy.

Job: Bank Clerk
Possible Presentation: Ten ways a safe-deposit box can save you money and convenience

Job: Lawyer
Possible Presentation: Cut your lawyer fees in half by using the law library and paralegals.

Job: Doctor
Possible Presentation: How to use your personal physician effectively to cut medical costs and remains healthy.

Job: Mugger
Possible Presentation: How muggers pick their victims and how not to be one.

If you've worked or done anything, you have skills. With creativity and boldness, you could catapult yourself into a whole new territory.

Teaching, speaking, and publishing are ways of drawing opportunities to you. When you showcase your skills, prospective buyers get to window shop—without a hard sell. And it's an avenue for obtaining individual clients and project contracts. If you're especially charismatic and persistent, and provide quality material, your talk, class or book could be a first step toward a consulting practice.

Chapter 20

STRATEGY
Connect

We get into the World Game when someone opens a door for us. Others hire us, buy our services, publish our papers, back us up, and invite us to join. Others teach and inspire us. It behooves you to connect with other people. Through connecting, we develop relationships and satisfy our longing to belong. Relationships can be stimulating, intimate, and supportive—they open doors. Let's look at some strategies for connecting.

Tactic—Network

Networking is a process that has been going on for centuries. Networking is what you do when you meet others at association meetings—to share stories, offer advice, give support, and make referrals. Networks provide a community, an in-group to which to belong. Seeking connections through a professional or social network is a time–tested strategy for locating the best prospects for a nonlinear move. All other things being equal, people will naturally select those they know for job appointments and consultation contracts.

Networking within your profession is good, but networking outside is a tactic of the astute. Expand your sphere of influence by connecting with people outside your area of expertise. Because you are unique, people notice and remember you. At the same time you learn valuable information about practices, problems, and trends in other specialties that may be helpful in your current work, as well as down the road in unexpected ways. As a rule of thumb, when you want to make a job change or move into a new field but don't know where to start—start by networking. Before you know it, opportunities appear and doors will open.

> The first step on the path of power is the assembling of a well-knit cadre, backed by followers.... In general, the magnitude of power in your hands is a direct function of the size of your constituency.... Until you have developed this necessary base, do not dream of going anywhere. Conversely, do not reach for power beyond the strength of the platform you have constructed.
>
> —R.G.H. Sui
> THE CRAFT OF POWER

Tactic—Show Belonging

It's not enough to simply place yourself in a setting. If you want to connect, you must do more. You must take the initiative. Consider the following situation. Imagine you are a guest at a party. What does a guest do? Guests stand around waiting to be introduced, feeling shy, and not knowing what to do. What does the host do? The host approaches newcomers, introduces them to others, and helps guests feel as if they belong.

The secret to effective connecting is to act as if the meeting is your party. Instead of waiting until someone says you belong, which is passive, approach people and initiate conversations. Introduce people to one another, like a host would, even if you've met them only moments before. Pull people into your conversations. Most people at social functions feel disconnected, like outsiders. Act as if you already belong. Everyone will like you—and remember you.

Tactic—Build Alliances

The way to get results in any organization is through alliances. Allies support you and speak up, saying, "That's a good idea," when you present a proposal, for example. Allies remove roadblocks so you can move forward and open doors so you can step inside.

It's essential, however, to remember that an alliance is a two–way street. Allies expect you to help them around roadblocks, too. Don't let them down. If you take too much from an ally for too long, you may soon have an adversary.

Find a Front Runner

Another tactic for getting support is to develop a " front–runner." For example, imbue an ally with your idea and encourage him or her to bring it up in the planning session. Then you function as the supporter of her idea. When two people are behind an idea, it has a greater chance of actualizing. You give up a little glory for having come up with the idea, but you achieve your objective.

Seek Allies at All Levels

Building alliances is the essence of teamwork. Develop allies in your immediate work group, in other sections of the organization as well as outside the company. Some of the best allies are to be found among secretaries and other support staff. They can clue you in to important gossip; they can make sure your work is completed accurately and on time; they can get you an audience with the boss; they can make you sound important by making calls for you.

Tactic—Become a Mentor

You've probably heard a lot about the importance of having a mentor, an advisor more seasoned than you who know the ropes. A mentor can alert you to the unstated dos and don'ts in your organization or profession and advise you on the most effective strategy to reach your goals. A mentor can mention your name in the right places, opening many doors.

But with so much emphasis on finding a mentor, we often neglect thinking about *becoming* mentors ourselves. Mentoring has many rewards. Much satisfaction is to be gained in guiding a junior, especially when our gems of wisdom are applied and succeed.

When a protégé excels, you as the mentor share the credit. You'll feel good and look good. Not only can a protégé bring enthusiasm, helping to revitalize your own, but often the junior has new ideas, new visions, and information about the latest technology and developments. Finally, being a mentor builds strong alliances that increase your sphere of influence and can be beneficial in unanticipated ways.

Chapter 21

STRATEGY
Transform

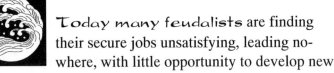 Today many feudalists are finding their secure jobs unsatisfying, leading nowhere, with little opportunity to develop new skills or to expand responsibilities. Millions of hard working feudalists are being "disintermediated"— replaced by white-collar robots that perform far better than they ever could—at a fraction of the price.

Ronin ride the waves and change themselves in the process. Rather than thinking of negative situations as hassles and problems, ronin accept that it is a time of doing ronin—accepting adversity as a test and discovering what it has to teach—how it can yield a benefit. In so doing they are no longer powerless before an oppressive situation—but empowered instead. In this way, adversity is transformed into an ally.

Tactic—Make It a Game

Thinking about work as a game changes your perspective, feelings, and eventually even your performance. But don't make the mistake of concluding that, because you call it a game, work is frivolous or unimportant. The Super Bowl is a game, but it certainly isn't frivolous. Millions of dollars are spent in preparing, playing, and televising it. Thinking of work as a game creates a degree of detachment that brings a broader perspective, enabling you to make better decisions.

What does "work is a game" mean? Play, sport, and amusement. Use these images as reminders to look for ways to derive fun from working. Being a game suggests a test of skill and competition with a winner or a goal to be achieved. Use this image as a reminder that work provides an opportunity to test your skill. A game involves an element of risk. Use this as a reminder to keep alert and to remember that in risk there is also adventure.

A game is played by the rules. Use this image to remember to uncover the rules so that you aren't disqualified. Winning a game involves strategy. Use this image to remind yourself to develop a contingency plan for using the rules, like an obstacle course, to the goal.

Tactic—Cultivate a Learner's Mind

In this time of tumultuous change the challenge is not what we need to learn but more what we need to *unlearn*. We must eliminate habits, practices and assumptions that once accounted for past successes to make room for new methods that better fit our circumstances.

> "Only as a warrior can one withstand the path of knowledge," Don Juan said. "A warrior cannot complain or regret anything. His life is an endless challenge, and challenges cannot possibly be good or bad. Challenges are simply challenges. The basic difference between an ordinary man and a warrior is that a warrior takes everything as a challenge." He went on, "while an ordinary man takes everything either as a blessing or as a curse."
>
> —*Carlos Castaneda*
> TALES OF POWER

Ironically, the more success we achieve as individuals and as organizations, the more difficult it is to change. We get stuck in repeating what worked in the past. This is natural and, up until now, was good for survival. What worked in the past will work again in the future has been a reliable rule of thumb. But when things change dramatically and all the rules go out the window—so does this guiding principle along with several others. In times of change, we must do new things in order to learn new methods. Repeating what worked in the past impedes learning new things.

Embrace Mistakes

Reflect on what you did well, what you did wrong. It is especially important to determine what you can learn from doing not so well. Question your habits of mind? We excel and grow by stretching our capabilities. Challenges and setting high performance goals are the technology for self-stretching. Don't play it safe, always doing only what you do well. Even when you are better than those around you are, you are not going anywhere, not learning anything new. This is how you can get stuck in your successes.

Kanji Secret

In Asian languages words are written with a symbol, or *kanji*. Sometimes two dissimilar *kanji*, when put together, have a meaning different from either of the separate components. The two *kanji* in the illustration stand for "trouble" and "gathering crisis." When combined, they mean "opportunity."

Gradual Redesign

Holding on to old ideas makes learning new ones difficult. Change is about reconceiving. When you reconceive an idea you recreate it and resee it in a new way. You put the pieces together in a new way—sometimes with a different background or foreground, for example. This is when change happens.

When we consider changing our lives we tend to view the process as being so dramatic, so earth shattering that any prospect of change, however small, seems overwhelming. So we avoid it and continue in the old way. This is a losing strategy when change is coming down upon us like a tidal wave. Holding firm to the past insures that we will be battered against the rocks.

Go with the Flow

Go with the flow of change so that instead of a major overhaul you gradually redesign. When you look at a old picture of your house you are probably struck by how it has changed—even though it feels pretty much the same. Perhaps there are different shrubs. Maybe you've added a deck or enclosed the porch. The house changed gradually. A garden path installed one year; a tree planted the next year. You didn't notice "a change!" It was just a gradual design with continual improvement through small incremental, seemingly insignificant steps. When you embrace change it can be just as easy. It doesn't have to be disruptive and traumatic—instead it flows naturally.

Incremental

Don't try to change everything at once. That would be like digging up your front and back yards, ripping down your garage and tearing off your roof. Instead focus on one or two significant habits or situations you want to increase or decrease. As you make progress, move on to the next "project." Just like improving your home is never really completed, you, too, are a work in progress.

All with whom we are associated can become our cooperators (without knowing it). For instance, a domineering superior or an exacting partner becomes as it were, the mental parallel bars on which our will...can develop its force and proficiency.... Talkative friends or time-wasters give us the chance to control speech, they teach us the art of courteous but firm refusal to engage in unnecessary conversation. To be able to say "no" is a difficult but useful discipline. So the Buddhist saying goes: "An enemy is as useful as a Buddha."

—Robert Assigioli
THE ART OF WILL

Find Practice Gyms

If there is an area in which you feel weak and incapable, find ways at work and at play to develop the needed skills. Any place where you can practice a skill is a "gym." A party is a place to practice listening or giving parts of a pitch, as an example. Seek ways to stretch yourself just a little. You could, for example, volunteer for an assignment you've never done before. Find practice gyms for yourself.

If you fear speaking in front of a group, find situations that require you to speak up and place yourself them. Don't let fear hold you back. Challenges help you shed old habits while opening doors to new vistas.

Tactic—Compete With Yourself

Competition is healthy. It motivates, spurring us on to reach new heights, to stretch our capabilities and push back our limits. In the process, we feel enthusiastic and develop confidence.

Competition, however, can become oppressive and downright stressful when it means competing with others to avoid losing—especially when our livelihood and professional reputation are at stake. Competition with others, when the stakes are high and losses severe, encourages us to focus on the gap between ourselves and our competitors, and to dwell on all the ways we don't match up.

Such detrimental competition can go to extremes, with people sabotaging one another by withholding information, being uncooperative, and backstabbing. Avoid this type of competition. Instead, an alternative is to compete with yourself. Use your past performance as the measure to surpass. Healthy competition like this is fun, invigorating, and motivating.

Use the Next-Time Rule

Most of us don't like failing. We forget that we learn by trying, making mistakes and trying again with a small correction. The enemy of good is trying to be perfect. When time is critical you have to make intelligent compromises without being able to weigh all the variables. Striving to be perfect paralyzes, preventing us from acting. To paraphrase Tom Peters, life is not about serenely walking down a spick and pan street. It is about veering to and fro, bouncing off the guardrails and then over correcting.

Watch yourself. Pay attention to your actions, to your work, to your performance. When you've performed poorly, stop and evaluate. Pay particular attention to what was good about it? Acknowledge yourself for that good performance. Determine what, specifically, could be improved. Don't criticize yourself, instead use the "next time rule." Determine the small improvement you will make next time. Rehearse the next time plan in your imagination.

The next time rule uses criticism and feedback positively to self-correct your course, while pushing you forward. When your performance is less than you hoped, consider it a challenge to overcome and a competitive standard to surpass. What improvement will you make next time? Remember to make it a small step.

Tactic—Find a Need and Fill It

In the cliché, "find a need and fill it," lies the secret of the next transformation. When unsatisfied at work, we tend to develop a negative focus, zeroing in on problems and bummers, quickly being seduced into a vicious cycle of negativity. Focusing on difficulties, we feel worse, our performance drops, and the problems become ever more oppressive.

Job market diagrams never include jobs for which no vacancy exists. It rarely occurs (to the job hunter) that if, instead (of looking for vacancies) he selects the organizations or companies that interest him, and does enough research to unearth their problems (and how he can help solve them) that they will be perfectly willing to create a new job for which no vacancy exists just because they will ultimately save money by doing so. (Problems always cost a lot more.)
—*Richard Bolles*
WHAT COLOR IS YOUR PARACHUTE

Problems signal that something is out of sync. Hidden in every problem is a need to be filled. Think of dissonant events as needs to be discovered and filled, rather than as bummers to be tolerated. By filling a need, you increase your visibility, feel more in control, expand job responsibilities, and become more valuable to those who need your skills.

Identify Needs

Be Alert. Open your eyes and look around. What problems do you notice at work? Focus on those touching you directly. These are the ones you are likely able to have an impact on. Keep notes on your observations. Periodically review the list of problems you've noticed. Take one or more that you find interesting and convert it into a statement of need.

Tactic—Make Friends at Work

Any work, no matter how routine, monotonous, or stressful, can be transformed by doing it with friends, people you feel good about, share parts of yourself with, and have fun with.

A number of years ago, a friend of mine invited me to a "Spring House Cleaning Party and Barbecue." I was amused by the idea and went because I felt like socializing. I hadn't realized however, the seriousness of her intention to have us guests clean her house. For two hours, we all labored away with a lot of enthusiasm, making jokes and laughing while cleaning her house from top to bottom. Afterward we drank beer and had a grand feast of barbecued hamburgers and franks.

Naturally, I was assigned to the bathroom. I never did like cleaning bathrooms, and I never knew anyone else who did either. As I scrubbed away at the toilet, with an ammonia filled sponge, wearing the rubber gloves she provided, I wondered, "What am I doing here cleaning this other person's toilet? Why aren't I home cleaning my own? The answer was simple: at home I'd be doing something dreary, alone with no friends to transform it into fun.

Make friends at work. Stop demanding that others always share your likes and dislikes. Instead, see what ways you can resonate with coworkers. With this approach, you can have a workable and enjoyable friendship with practically any person. When you look forward to going to work to see friends, working will be transformed.

Tactic—Create Balance

Industrialization with its demand for extreme specialization has created an imbalanced work style that we have come to consider "normal". The disharmony in our lives is often so extreme that balance seems impossible, even abnormal.

This is the world of the workaholic, devoting herself to work at the expense of all else. This is the world of the specialist, who cannot communicate with anyone not intimately acquainted with his esoteric knowledge. This is the world of repetitive work. This is the world of corporate feudalism.

Listen to Feedback

How do we know when we are losing balance? There are two indicators: what others say and how we feel. Feedback from those around us is a mirror. Criticism and compliments are the reflection. Reflection from others is a valuable gem—a gift. Reflection offers a check of where we are and how we stand. Are we succeeding or failing? Are we acceptable or unacceptable?

We each live inside our own reality. What we do, how we act, how we think, what we like, or what we don't like all make perfect sense to us. We cannot escape our own minds.

We interpret everything in terms of personal reality. We can never get outside ourselves to see ourselves as others do—except a little bit through feedback.

Many reject the gift of feedback by punishing the giver with defensiveness and attacks, or by ignoring it. Foolish! Why should someone continue to give gifts? Don't do this. You need reflections from the world, especially in times of change, don't close it off. Instead, listen to what others say. Encourage them. Ask questions, and actively seek feedback.

Listening to others does not mean you must accept what they say. But you can't decide if what they say is valid or invalid unless you listen first. You need not have a knee–jerk reaction, shutting it all out. Be autonomous instead. Take what is useful, discard the rest.

If others say, in jest or seriousness, that you're working excessively, for example, or goofing off or spending too much money, or being too stubborn, or drinking a lot—listen. Feedback is also a lighthouse beacon. Look to see if you are getting close to the rocks.

Check Feelings

The second balance indicator is feelings of satisfaction or dissatisfaction. Dissatisfaction is a warning that something is wrong, that there is an imbalance—you are not receiving something you need or you are doing something too much. Dissatisfaction is your psychological tummy saying, "I'm hungry. Feed me. Feed me."

There is no one feeling, no one thought to watch for. It helps to record your feelings and thoughts in a notebook or journal. When you have many notations, review them. Look beyond the specific thoughts or feelings for a pattern of imbalance.

When you were a child struggling first to ride a two–wheeler, you quickly learned to avoid extreme shifts and to make many rapid counter–balancing adjustments instead. By mastering balance on a physical level, you learned to ride at high speeds on two thin wheels and were no longer restricted to walking.

There are many more secrets to balance to be learned and transformations to be uncovered. Each time you experience dissatisfaction or receive disturbing feedback, remember it is an opportunity to learn more about the magic of balance, just as each fall from your two wheeler taught you more about how to ride.

Know What's Enough

In the old feudal workplace success is defined by economic bracket and job level. Many movers and shakers are increasingly dissatisfied as they find themselves on a treadmill and getting nowhere they really want to go. Increasingly we are questioning what do we "really" want to do with the rest of our lives which brings us to the issue of "enoughness" and designing a life that works.

What is satisfaction? It seems like a simple enough question. Yet, most of us have a surprisingly difficult time finding the answer. So we stay on the treadmill. Either we determine for ourselves what we find fulfilling—or it will be defined for us. Up until now we have been buying other's notions of what we want.

It is one of those ying/yang-type question. Hand-in-hand with figuring out what is fulfilling is figuring out what is enough—when are you satiated. Knowing *when* you are satisfied is as important as knowing *what* is satisfying. Not having a measure of enough has been likened to a hungry dog that, if permitted, will eat until it collapses.

Figuring out your satisifiers and how much of them it takes has little to do with money. Money blinds us and we go for it like the bull charging the red flag. In and of itself, money has no inherent value. It is the medium we use to obtain what we want—or think we want. When we focus on money as a satisfier, we are ripe for exploitation because we become indentured—willing to do anything for money. But when we get it, it is never enough—it doesn't bring the satisfaction we imagined and so we hunger for yet more money in the hopes that this time we will feel full. Identifying satisfers begins with questions like, "What do I love doing?" and "What do I want to 'spend' my time on?"

Hungry Ghost

The Buddhist warn of the hungry ghost with a huge belly and a mouth so tiny that it can never get enough so is always wanting more. Many ronin discover that they too have a hungry ghost inside. This was especially apparent among the IPO millionaires and the dot-com high fliers who had more wealth than many kingdoms of old. As Elizabeth Gibson-Meier observed, they were still unsatisfied and driven by an unknown, insatiable desire. Nothing they accomplish was enough.

Answering a question of how much is enough is not something you do just once, it is something to ponder from time to time. What feels right today will change. It is amazingly difficult to pin point what we really want. But when we do, then we know what to strive for. When we know what we want we can develop a compelling image of our achieving it. That image acts like a magnet that draws you to what you want.

Chapter 22

STRATEGY
Boomerang

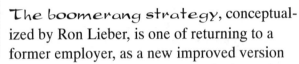 The boomerang strategy, conceptualized by Ron Lieber, is one of returning to a former employer, as a new improved version of your old self with deeper skills and broader know how. Having worked there before, you have something special to offer—you know "how we do things around here." You know key people and you have a network in place. You are already one of the club.

Tactic—Leave Well

How well you leave has an enormous impact on the possibility of a return act. Your exit behavior is remembered long after your contributions are forgotten. If your departure was contentious, returning is vastly more difficult. Even if you hate the place along with everyone there, why reduce your options by leaving poorly? When you act like a jerk, you kill any chance of going back.

Even though you may feel like doing so, do not vent. Overcome the urge to give a sermon to your supervisor on his lousy management skills. You never know. Companies merge, things change, supervisors advance to positions of greater power. So leave by the high road with them remembering what you contributed. Leave well and you will get better references while leaving the door open for future possibilities.

Do Just a Little More

It is pretty easy; all you have to do is a little more than the minimal expected. You might give more than two weeks notice, for example, especially if you shoulder a lot of responsibility. Make sure all your projects are wrapped up and offer to show your successor how to handle every aspect of the job. If you don't train your replacement, leave detailed written instructions with your phone number or email address. You will get a lot of mileage from doing this.

Tactic—Stay in Orbit

Lifetime employment with one company is a thing of the past while lifetime affiliation is something we're likely to see more often. The idea is to stay in orbit in such a way that you maintain contact with the pulse of the company. Most obvious is the importance of maintaining relationships with former co-workers and supervisors. Not only will this help you keep up on what's happening, but also they can alert you to new directions and potential openings. Don't expect them to initiate. You'll need to make the initial efforts; after all you are the one who left.

Jobs and functions are no longer the rigid pre-formed boxes found on feudal organizational charts. Today functions are elastic and jobs are shaped by their holders. Being employed is no longer an all or nothing arrangement. If, for example, you provide a valuable service that is not easily replaced, you may be able to redefine your relationship into an ongoing consulting position. Maybe you can become a vendor providing the same services you provide now as an employee—only as a subcontractor which can save the company a bundle in benefits, tax co-payments, and overhead. You may be able to put a little of that bundle into your pocket. And, with your former employer as the cornerstone of your new operation, it'll be easier to get other customers to sign on. Another possibility is to relocate your office into your house and work online from home. Many relationships are possible.

Tactic—Articulate Your Motives

Before taking concrete steps to go back it is important to identify why you left in the first place. If you left under a cloud or were pushed out after being passed over, think carefully before returning. What happened before is likely to happen again. What makes you think it will be different a second time around?

It is important to be able to articulate your motivation for going back. If it's negatively propelled such as the new job is not working out, it is wise to hold off. Your old employer will want to know why you left, why you want to return and if you can be trusted to stick around. The old company will always be concerned about trust. You need to show that your return is not a retreat but an advance for you as well as for the employer. Prepare for this. When you have clarified your motivation and can state it succinctly you will be better able to be convincing during the interview process. It can help to get feedback from a trusted insider. Call people whose opinion you respect and who have insight into the company's current climate.

Tactic—Repackage Yourself

Most likely the old company has changed and you will have catching up to do. Don't go riding in on a high horse with an attitude that you've learned a lot and are coming back to fix their problems. Better to find out how your old colleagues and supervisors have changed and what they have learned before determining your approach.

Just as you may be seeing the company as it was before, so too will you have to get your old co-workers to see the new you. You'll need a plan for being different without being defensive. Expect co-workers to interact with you pretty much in the same way as they did during your first tour of duty. The tendency will be to fall back into the old dance—it will come naturally because you already know the steps and follow the lead. If you and a particular co-worker were a "gruesome twosome," for example, that person is likely to expect to step right back into that relationship.

Develop a plan for handling each person individually. It's best to set the stage to take a different role beforehand. Then take the lead yourself. Suppose, for example, you went to lunch everyday with Bill. When you see Bill, you can use your "lines." For example, you might say, "Hey, I'm really looking forward to sharing time with you and catching up on all the gossip. Let's do a light dinner at Andy's after work. These days I do lunch at the gym—gotta keep the old heart in shape. Catch you at 5, okay?" You might even role-play the encounter with your spouse or a friend.

PART FOUR
CORPORATE RONIN

Chapter 23

Corporate Change

 Innovation usually pivots around what Peters and Waterman in their ground breaking report, *In Search of Excellence*, call a "product champion"—a fanatic who inspires extra effort and pushes the product through the bureaucratic maze. It is in the nature of corporations to squelch this process because such a ronin style is viewed as at odds with the way that businesses manage employees. Ronin are regarded as too independent, and much of what they do is seen as challenging the status quo. Consequently, their corporate lives are filled with many hurdles and few rewards for overcoming them. It is almost as if organizations unwittingly conspire to kill the spirit of the ronin they so desperately need.

> *The most discouraging fact of big corporate life is the loss of what got them big in the first place: innovation.*
> —*Peters and Waterman*
> *In Search of Excellence*

Rigid By Design

The very structure of organizations discourages innovation. Mechanisms meant to keep the organization on its planned course inhibit change and entrepreneurialism in the process. For example, functions are compartmentalized into specialties and arranged into chains of command that create barriers to communication. Internal controls are set into place to reduce risk, but the result is that organizations forget how to experiment and adapt. When innovations do emerge, they are less likely to be used.

Traditional organizations are replete with rules that fence us in. As protocol takes precedence over performance, corporate fiefdoms defend themselves by using rules to withhold information, resources, and support needed to get the job done.

Because innovation in feudal systems requires going against the grain, it is not too surprising that most innovations in traditional organizations come from newcomers, outsiders, or malcontents who do the wrong thing, in the wrong place at the wrong time. Such corporate feudalism produces a rigidity that is a disaster in an era of rapidly accelerating change. By comparison, innovative companies adapt by shifting posture and resources as circumstances require and thereby stay ahead of change.

> *The corporations that will succeed and flourish in the times ahead will be those that have mastered the art of change, creating a climate encouraging the introduction of new procedures and new possibilities, encouraging anticipation of and response to external pressures, encouraging and listening to new ideas from inside the organization.*
>
> *The individuals who will succeed and flourish will also be masters of change: adept at reorienting their own and others' activities in untried directions to bring about higher levels of achievement. They will be able to acquire and use power to produce innovation.*
>
> —*Rosabeth Moss Kanter*
> *THE CHANGE MASTERS*

Routinizing

The primary function of a hierarchy is to maintain the organization and its production. By routinizing useful procedures, a hierarchy defines titles, pay, reporting relationships and tasks. Opportunities tend to be limited to formal promotional paths in which power follows position.

> By necessity for efficiency reasons some jobs have a high component of routine, repetitive do it as ordered action. . . . The problem for innovaiton and change is not the existence of such tasks but the confinement of some people within them.
> —*Rosabeth Moss Kanter*
> *THE CHANGE MASTERS*

Kanter says that innovation comes out of successfully grappling with the challenge of combining the necessity for routine jobs with the possibility of employee participation beyond these jobs. She seeing the ideal compromise being for a "mechanistic production hierarchy" and a "participative problem solving organization" to exist side by side, carrying out different but complementary types of tasks.

Parallel Structures

The participative problem solving organizations Kanter studied are oriented toward change. In these organizations, she observed fluidity that allows people to be grouped temporarily in a number of different ways, as appropriate to the problem solving tasks at hand. In this "parallel structure" as Kanter calls it, opportunity and power can be expanded far beyond what is available in the regular hierarchal organization. The parallel structure exists simultaneously with hierarchy, not replacing it but rather serving different purposes—to examine routines, to explore new options, and to develop new tools, procedures, and approaches. And as the utility of new routines is demonstrated, they are transferred to the line organization for maintenance and integration.

In short, according to Kanter's findings, to be innovative organizations must have two ways of arranging people. First they need hierarchy with specified tasks and functional groupings for carrying out what they already know how to do and can anticipate will be done in the same way in the future. But organizations also need a set of flexible vehicles for figuring out how to do what they don't yet know, such as how to encourage entrepreneurs and how to engage both the grass roots and the elite in mastering innovation.

How. . . could the mind of the strategist, with its inventive Èlan, be reproduced in [the]corporate cultures? What were the ingredients of an excellent strategist? . . . the answer I came up with involved the formation within the corporation a group of young "samurais" who would play a duel role. On the one hand they would function as real strategists, giving free rein to their imagination and entrepreneurial flair in order to come up with bold and innovative strategic ideas. On the other hand, they would serve as staff analysts, testing out, digesting, and assigning priorities to the ideas, and providing staff assistance to line managers in implementing the approved strategies. This "samurai" concept has since been adapted in several Japanese firms with great success.

—*Kenichi Ohmae*
The Mind of the Strategist

Roots of Innovation

More than the people working within it, the environment of the organization makes the biggest difference in the amount of innovative activity. Innovative organizations are characterized by open communication that promotes sharing ideas and solving problems; relationship ties that cut across functions, levels, and departments, and decentralization of resources. Experimentation, the most powerful catalyst for getting innovation into action, must be encouraged, and the failures that inevitably result must be accepted.

Multidiscipline Teams

Innovation thrives best in environments in which small groups of people, usually ten or fewer, work together. Small work units promote increased participation and better communication as well as feelings of commitment and ownership over projects. In fact, small work places outperform big ones on almost every performance indicator. But not just any small group of people working together produces innovation. Groups function best and are most productive when they consist of volunteers from a variety of fields who set their own goals for a project of limited duration.

Support Systems

Rich support systems are needed to counteract the organization's built-in opposition to change. Circulating people across jobs allows people to learn a number of skills, while facilitating the formation of networks. The complex ties that develop encourage employees to cut across job boundaries to work collectively with others. Companies benefit by a flexible and adaptable work force, and employees gain from added variety and the challenge of learning.

Intrepreneuring

One way of bringing more of the entrepreneurial spirit into the corporation is through "intrepreneuring" by establishing a company within the corporation. Although in the strictest sense, the intrepreneur stays an employee, special rules govern the

The Intrepreneur

The [intrepreneur] is allowed great freedom of action. . . . Once the business plan is accepted he can "borrow" corporate money at a stated interest rate. He can buy services from corporate staff or outsiders as he wishes, or rent office space elsewhere if it is cheaper than the available space, or hire full-time staff people from corporate staff departments. The only limits are that he adhere to standard corporate accounting procedures and use corporate lawyers.

—*Copulsky and McNulty*
ENTREPRENEURSHIP AND THE CORPORATION

interplay between the intrepreneur and the corporation. The objective is to simulate a small business environment. This innovative approach promises to combine the advantages of the large organization and the entrepreneurial venture.

Chapter 24

Ronin as Company Asset

 Innovation is not a step-by-step, carefully planned linear process. True, during planning a target or direction is identified, but getting there is much like sailing. Unable to sail straight into the wind, the captain navigates generally north by northeast, then correcting the course as the boat comes about, and tacking to the northwest. Likewise, we will not solve the riddles of living in an organizational world with a linear approach. We must experiment and make mistakes to discover and refine new ways of doing things.

Strategic Thinking

The acts of a myriad of individuals drive the innovative organization. There would be no innovation without someone somewhere deciding to shape and push an idea until it takes usable form as a new product, management system, or work method. Corporate ronin create new possibilities for organizational action by testing limits and by pushing and directing the innovative process. They have an intellectual elasticity and performance flexibility that enables them to come up with realistic responses to changing situations.

See the Big Picture

Ronin bring many benefits to the corporation. As a result of nonlinear moves and a range of experience and skill they tend to see problems in a larger perspective and understand how the important operations of the company come together. They bring ideas and material from different corners together in new ways. Having moved laterally within the company, Ronin have allies in different departments and at different levels, enabling them to build coalitions to get things done.

What distinguishes the Maverick Executive from all executives is his rare constellation of characteristics, skills, attitudes, strengths, and weaknesses. His most notable marks are exceptional drive, courage, optimism, and decisiveness. But a listing of his features would also embrace an extraordinary diversity of terms many paradoxical: excitable and tireless, self-confident and intolerant, suspicious and gullible, decisive and nonanalytical, dedicated and fickle, superficial and profound, persevering and nonconforming, autocratic and versatile, inspiring and ruthless, indifferent and meddling, impetuous and rigid, obsessive and careless, scheming and unreflective, demanding and casual, critical and idolizing.

—Robert N. McNulty
THE MAVERICK EXECUTIVE

Bend the Rules

Ronin envision new possibilities, and when organizational structure and protocol block actualizing their vision, they are inclined to bend the rules. For example, they have been known to transfer finds from one budget line to another, act before they receive official approval, and bootleg resources. It's this characteristic that ronin are not beholden to the traditional rules, to The Company Way that organizations both fear and desperately need.

Lone Rangers

A small number of entrepreneurs in unreceptive environments are what Ken Farbstein called "Lone Rangers", organization loyalists acing on their values to remedy what they see as less than optimum situations for a company and a job they care about. The person who is this kind of "bureaucratic insurgent" can be an activist reformer who remains loyal to the organization and its mission while working gradually but persistently to "convert the heathen.... He takes advantage of loopholes, skirts the edge of regulations, evades formal orders, and is less than fully complacent when he cannot ignore them."

Half outlaw as well as hero, [the] innovator may be ready to break the rules to reach a greater goal. He or she may engage in illicit budget transfers using funds fir a purpose other than the official one, holding offsite meetings to raise the morale of troops even though the company has forbidden it, create his or her own rewards systems, spend money before it is allocated or even get a product into production before receiving official approval.

—*Rosabeth Moss Kanter*
The Change Master

Make Things Happen

Corporate ronin shape their jobs. They know how to use power, and they can mobilize people and resources to get things done. Ronin are self-directed. When infused with purpose, corporate ronin will take it upon themselves to damn the bureaucracy and maneuver their projects through the system. They set their own goals, and take personal responsibility for solving problems and feedback.

Ronin and Company Profits

Ronin contribute to company profits in three ways: productivity, innovation and adaptability.

Productivity

Being self-starters and working for goals they have defined, autonomous employees offer high productivity potential. This potential can translate into company profits if their greater motivation is harnessed and directed with the proper management strategy.

Innovation

The second way ronin contribute to profits is through innovation. Their diversified experience combined with strategic thinking increases innovative breakthroughs, such as the discovery of profitable loopholes.

Adaptability

The third way ronin contribute to company profits is through adaptability, being able to respond creatively to changes in technology and the marketplace. Their diversified experience and transferable skills enable them to assume a variety of roles as needed, and their creativity encourages finding workable alternatives.

> *The potential exists for an American corporate Renaissance, with its implied return to greatness. Because recent economic conditions have been so unfavorable for American business, leaders should be motivated to search for new solutions and to engage their entire work force in the search. I argue that innovation is the key. Individuals can make a difference, but they need the tools and the opportunity to use them. They need to work in settings where they are valued and supported, their intelligence given a chance to blossom. They need to have the power to be able to take the initiative to innovate.*
>
> —*Rosabeth Moss Kanter*
> THE CHANGE MASTERS

In times of transition, a ronin archetype appears as part of the endless cycle of stagnation and rebirth. With ronin lies hope for a Corporate Renaissance, because they have the potential to stimulate innovation and revitalize the corporation. Harnessing this potential is the challenge managers face.

Many of the factors that have been stifling productivity and job satisfaction are being superceded by new structures. Confusion and uncertainty will inevitably accompany this transition.

Chapter 25

Become a
Corporate Ronin

First ronin experiences are often in response to practical factors in the work environment. For example, sometimes we begin to exhibit ronin qualities when confronted with a job that is just too large. Carving out a concrete goal requires an innovative approach. Other times, jobs are too small and we are bored and unfulfilled. Another common spur to becoming a ronin is realizing that advancement is blocked.

Operating within a large organization without burning out or becoming an indentured, interchangeable part is no small feat.

Doris Randall . . . was the new head of the backwater purchasing department that she feared would join personnel and public relations as the "three Ps" of women's ghettoized job assignments in the electronics industry. But she eventually parlayed technical information from users of the department's services into an agreement from her boss to allow her to make the first wave of changes. No one in her position had ever had such close contact with users before, and Randall found this a potent basis for reorganizing her unit into a set of user oriented specialties, with each staff member concentrating on a particular user need. Once the system was in place, and hers acknowledged to be functioning as the best purchasing department in the region, she went on to expand this kind of reorganization into other two purchasing departments in the division.

—Rosabeth Moss Kanter
THE CHANGE MASTERS

On the other hand, within organizations lies opportunity. They provide a competitive arena in which to expand experience, to develop capabilities, to pursue adventure, and to attain excellence. Working in a corporation poses a challenge that develops and hones up skills. Operating in a corporation is a true warrior's test.

Negotiating Paradox

Working in an organization means contending with contradiction. Turning these paradoxes to your advantage is an adventure in becoming a warrior. The *Way of the Ronin* is guided by the code of autonomy—directing oneself, excellence—carrying out the right action, and adaptability—remaining flexible.

Individual Contributor vs. Team Member

The first corporate paradox is the inherent contradiction between your roles as an individual and as a member of a work group. Inevitably, work within an organization is a team activity, involving groups of people working together to achieve goals. Yet, ronin tend toward the extreme of individualism.

The need to be a good team member and the propensity toward individualism make the corporation an excellent opportunity for ronin to wrestle with the shadows of meism, opportunism, and glibness. And it is an opportunity to learn to synergize and direct group efforts.

Those who succumb to individualism are often ejected from the game not for poor work but for being poor team players. Others who fail to resolve the paradox are slowly seduced into becoming indentured. Loyalty to the team is transformed into seeking approval and acceptance instead of striving for excellence.

Resolution

The resolution of the paradox is achieved by utilizing the golden mean to determine the excellent action. The middle point between independence and dependence is autonomy and interdependence. Autonomy is different from independence. It means self-direction, whereas independence means not dependent. In day-to-day interactions autonomy is exercised through ongoing choices between being a rebel and standing up for what you believe versus conforming and going along.

Innovation vs. Regulation

The second paradox is the contradiction between assigned project goals and corporate demands that emanate from bureaucracy and politics. Everyone who works in an organization comes up against this contradiction. It is the damned-if-you-do, damned-if-you-don't bind that undermines motivation and contributes to job burnout. This paradox is particularly difficult for ronin, who are motivated by striving toward the accomplishment of project goals and become agitated when their goals must be placed second to The Company Way. When this happens, ronin are tempted to bend the rules and often do.

Resolution

This paradox is resolved by exercising wisdom in using general knowledge of the situation and its dynamics to develop a strategy or plan of action. Wisdom is knowing ways to breakthrough log jams and to open windows of opportunity in The Company Way, such as redefining goals as compatible, using higher corporate goals to supercede lower ones, going to the meta level, identifying loopholes, or making an end run. Wisdom directs the development of tactics, the practical steps for implementing the plan.

Diversify vs. Specialize

The third paradox ronin must negotiate is the concurrent pressures to both diversify and specialize.

Through the promotional track and job labeling, organizations push us into specializing. Yet when we specialize, we simultaneously limit our upward movement, because top management positions require diversity and broad vision.

Resolution

The resolution to this paradox is achieved by using nonlinear planning to become a generalist with specialties. Follow the strategies of moving indirectly and concentrated dispersion described earlier.

> *Broad diversified experience in all the important operations of a company us becoming the primary qualification for upper level jobs.... Your long range strategy must incorporate lateral moves to get the experience which paves the way upward. For all...who have been locked into a narrow corner of their field, the smartest way to promote yourself and your career is to move sideways...the shortest path to the top is not straight up, it is a zigzag field run.*
>
> *—Betty Lehan Harragan*
> GAMES MOTHER NEVER TAUGHT YOU

Rigidity vs. Oscillation

There is comfort and security in stability—sameness. We know what to expect and everything has a place. But sameness leads to stagnation and boredom. The world does not remain the same. At the other extreme lies constant change. When we attempt to adjust to all aspects of change at once we begin to oscillate and become frantic. Some pursue change for change sake, regardless if it is needed or of what might be disrupted. Constant change gives the illusion of motion, of going somewhere when it may be running away. Constant change can be an avoidance of grappling with the challenge of creating stability and building something lasting.

Resolution

The resolution is to go with the flow. Make small, incremental changes in response to circumstances. The smallness of the changes allows for stability and our anxieties are not triggered. Yet, small constant changes can be transformative. Recall the example of slowly fixing up your house over years. A new deck. A fence. Plant a tree. Add a room. When you look at a photo of your house 10 or 15 years ago, the changes are dramatic. Yet, when made slowly, in small projects, they were easy to make and easy to adjust to.

A Great and Yeasty Time

As Naisbitt said, this is a yeasty time— the time of the parenthesis. For ronin, it is a time of exciting possibilities—a time of adventure.

We are living in the time of the parenthesis, the time between eras. Those who are willing to handle the ambiguity of this in-between period and to anticipate the new era will be a quantum leap ahead of those who hold on to the past. The time of the parenthesis is a time of change and questioning. Although the time between eras is uncertain, it is a great and yeasty time, filled with opportunity. If we can learn to make uncertainty our friend, we can achieve much more than in stable eras. In stable eras, everything has a name, and everything knows its place, and we can leverage very little. But in the time of the parenthesis we have extraordinary leverage and influence—individually, professionally, and institutionally— if we can only get a clear sense, a clear conception, a clear vision, of the road ahead. My God, what a fantastic time to be alive!

—John Naisbitt

MEGATRENDS

Index

Books by Docpotter

OVERCOMING JOB BURNOUT
HOW TO RENEW ENTHUSIASM FOR WORK

FINDING A PATH WITH A HEART
HOW TO GO FROM

FROM CONFLICT TO COOPERATION
HOW TO RESOLVE A DISPUTE

DR. BEVERLY POTTER
High Performance Goal Setting

The Worrywart's Companion
Twenty-one Ways to

HEALING MAGIC OF CANNABIS

BRAIN BOOSTERS

TURNING AROUND

DRUG TESTING
A GUIDE FOR EMPLOYERS
AT WORK

REVISED EDITION
PREVENTING JOB BURNOUT
Transforming Work Pressures Into Productivity
Beverly A. Potter, Ph.D.
Eight Proven Strategies to Beat Job Burnout

PASS THE TEST
AN EMPLOYEE GUIDE TO DRUG TESTING
Beverly A. Potter, Ph.D.
J. Sebastian Orfali, M.A.

About Docpotter

Dr. Beverly Potter's work blends the philosophies of humanistic psychology, Eastern mysticism with principles of behavior psychology to create an inspiring approach to handling the many challenges encountered in today's workplace.

Docpotter earned her masters of science in vocational rehabilitation counseling from San Francisco State and her doctorate in counseling psychology from Stanford University. She was a member of the Stanford Staff Development team for 18 years, has taught at the graduate level and is a dynamic and informative speaker. Her workshops have been sponsored by numerous colleges, corporations, associations and governmental agencies. She has authored many books and is best known for her work on job burnout.

Docpotter's website is docpotter.com and is loaded with useful information. Please visit.

Eric O'Connell/People Magazine

Ronin Books for Independent Minds

OVERCOMING JOB BURNOUT .... Potter OVEJOB 14.95 ___
  How to renew enthusiasm for work-includes burnout tests.

THINK FOR YOURSELF! .... Presley THIFOR 13.95 ___
  Questioning pressure to conform, independent thinking test..

HIGH PERFORMANCE GOAL SETTING .... Potter HIGOAL 9.95 ___
  How to use intuition to conceive and achieve your dreams.

LIVING CHEAPLY WITH STYLE .... Callenbach LCHEAP 13.95 ___
  Tips on how to stretch a dollar while adding to quality of life.

FINDING A PATH WITH A HEART .... Potter FINPAT 14..95 ___
  How to go from burnout to bliss, principles of self-leading.

YOUR BRAIN IS GOD .... Leary YOUBRA 10.95 ___
  Do-it-yourself-religion by Timothy Leary.

FROM CONFLICT TO COOPERATION .... Potter FROCON 14.95 ___
  How to mediate a dispute, step-by-step technique.

ILLUMINI PAPERS .... Wilson ILLPAP 14.95 ___
  Robert Anton Wilson's rants and visions. A classic.

CHAOS & CYBERCULTURE .... Leary CHACYB 29.95 ___
  Tim Leary's magnus opus on the past, present and future.

BRAIN BOOSTERS .... Potter & Orfali BRABOO 16.95 ___
  Foods & drugs that make you smarter.

(When ordering by phone, use book code in CAPITAL LETTERS just to the left of price)

Books prices: **SUBTOTAL**	$_____
Money order discount 10% (USA only)	_____
CA customers add sales tax 8.25%	_____
BASIC SHIPPING: (All orders)	**$4.00**

PLUS SHIPPING: USA+$1 for each book, Canada+$2 for each book,
{ Europe+$7 for each book, Pacific+$10 for each book }
  Books + Tax + Basic + Shipping: TOTAL $_____

Checks payable to **Ronin Publishing** (For 10% Off Use Money Order — USA only)

MC _ Visa _ Exp date __ - __ card #: _ _ _ _ _ _ _ _ _ _ _ _ _ _ _ (sign) _ _ _ _ _ _ _ _ _ _ _ _

Name_ _

Address _ _ _ _ _ _ _ _ _ _ _ _ _ _ _ _ _ _ City _ _ _ _ _ _ _ _ _ _ State _ _ _ ZIP _ _ _ _ _ _

PRICE & AVAILABILITY SUBJECT TO CHANGE WITHOUT NOTICE.

☞ Call us anytime for our FREE catalog On-line catalog— roninpub.com

℃ **Orders (800)858-2665 • Info (510)420-3669 • Fax (510)420-3672**
Available at amazon.com or order through your independent bookstore.
Ask your library to add *The Way of the Ronin* **to their collection.**